A GUIDE FOR **BOLD,**

WE CAN'T
TALK
ABOUT
THAT

Second
Edition

AT WORK!

HOW TO TALK ABOUT
RACE, RELIGION, POLITICS,
AND OTHER POLARIZING TOPICS

MARY-FRANCES WINTERS
and MAREISHA N. REESE

BK·

Berrett–Koehler Publishers, Inc.

Berrett-Koehler Publishers, Inc.
1333 Broadway, Suite 1000, Oakland, CA 94612-1921
Tel: (510) 817-2277; Fax: (510) 817-2278; www.bkconnection.com

ORDERING INFORMATION

Quantity sales. Special discounts are available on quantity purchases by corporations,
associations, and others. For details, contact the "Special Sales Department" at the
Berrett-Koehler address above.

Individual sales. Berrett-Koehler publications are available through most bookstores.
They can also be ordered directly from Berrett-Koehler: Tel: (800) 929-2929; Fax:
(802) 864-7626; www.bkconnection.com.

Orders for college textbook/course adoption use. Please contact Berrett-Koehler:
Tel: (800) 929-2929; Fax: (802) 864-7626.

Distributed to the US trade and internationally by Penguin Random House Publisher
Services.

Berrett-Koehler and the BK logo are registered trademarks of Berrett-Koehler
Publishers, Inc.

All graphics by The Winters Group, Inc., unless otherwise cited.

Printed in the United States of America

Berrett-Koehler books are printed on long-lasting acid-free paper. When it is available, we choose paper that has been manufactured by environmentally responsible
processes. These may include using trees grown in sustainable forests, incorporating
recycled paper, minimizing chlorine in bleaching, or recycling the energy produced at
the paper mill.

Library of Congress Cataloging-in-Publication Data
    Names: Winters, Mary-Frances, author. | Reese, Mareisha N., author.
    Title: We can't talk about that at work! : how to talk about race, religion, politics,
and other polarizing topics / Mary-Frances Winters, Mareisha N. Reese.
    Other titles: We cannot talk about that at work!
    Description: Second Edition. | Oakland, CA : Berrett-Koehler Publishers, [2024] |
Revised edition of We can't talk about that at work!, [2017] | Includes bibliographical
references and index.
    Identifiers: LCCN 2023037808 (print) | LCCN 2023037809 (ebook) |
ISBN 9781523006311 (paperback) | ISBN 9781523006328 (pdf) |
ISBN 9781523006335 (epub)
    Subjects: LCSH: Communication in organizations. | Interpersonal communica-
tion. | Interpersonal relations. | Organizational sociology.
    Classification: LCC HD30.2 .W5636 2024 (print) | LCC HD30.2 (ebook) | DDC
650.1/3—dc23
    LC record available at https://lccn.loc.gov/2023037808
    LC ebook record available at https://lccn.loc.gov/2023037809

SECOND EDITION

31 30 29 28 27 26 25 24 23 || 10 9 8 7 6 5 4 3 2 1
Book producer: BookMatters
Cover designer: Daniel Tesser

To the generations of freedom fighters, civil rights leaders, and social justice advocates who preceded us in the ongoing quest for an inclusive, equitable, and just world that values the dignity of all people.

And especially to those who lost their lives in the struggle. Without their sacrifice, our voices would not be possible.

Contents

Polarization Persists Today

Note on terms: Language describing various identity groups is ever changing. There is no universal agreement, and, in our attempt to be respectful of different perspectives, we acknowledge that the terms we have chosen may not resonate with all readers. The term **BIPOC*** *(Black, Indigenous, and people of color) is used in the book to recognize that while every identity has had its unique journey with racism, there are shared experiences that we attempt to capture. When not citing language directly from a study or quote, we use* **Latine** *to describe individuals who have historically been identified as Hispanic, Latino, or Latinx. Latine, created by* **LGBTQIA+** *Spanish speakers, adopts the letter e from the Spanish language to represent gender neutrality.[1]* **SWANA** *is a decolonized term for the Southwest Asian/North African region that was created by its own community members to be used instead of names that are Eurocentric in origin, such as the Middle East or Near East.[2]*

Note on capitalization: We capitalize Black and lowercase white when referring to these two identity groups to follow

---

*Words in the text that are **sans serif bold** are defined in the glossary.

Brookings's decision to change its style guide in this way. Brookings cites rationale from the New York Times *dating back to 1930: "It is an act in recognition of racial respect for those who have been generations in the 'lower case.'"*[3]

◆ ◆ ◆

We still can't talk about that at work!

We are so pleased to coauthor the second edition of *We Can't Talk about That at Work!* In this update, Mareisha N. Reese, president and chief operating officer of The Winters Group, Inc., adds her voice from the perspective of a xennial (cusp of millennial and Generation X). We include new research, resources, and examples. In addition, we added a chapter with experiences from two organizations that are effectively using the Bold, Inclusive Conversations model developed by Mary-Frances Winters. We also include a discussion guide.

When the first edition of *We Can't Talk about That at Work!* came out in 2017, we had already come to realize that there was a great deal of **polarization** around sociopolitical issues that impeded our ability to have civil discourse about our different perspectives. It is evident to most of us that we are even more polarized today. Since the first edition, extreme views on issues like reproductive rights, gender identity, gun control, climate change, immigration, and the age-old issue of race and racism have increased. We have witnessed the reversal of *Roe v. Wade,* a fifty-year-old Supreme Court decision that gave women the right to abortions; state legislation restricting the teaching of the history of racism in schools and the workplace; legislation that denies transgender individuals equal rights; and restrictions on workplace diversity training and more. We think we can all agree that we need the skills to effectively discuss some of the most pressing issues of our time that impact workers everywhere.

We are in the throes of culture wars that directly impact the workplace in many ways, including what we need to talk about and how to talk about these issues. We continue to see vast divisions that exacerbate an "us-and-them" disunity—many of the issues are political in nature involving legislative action that is further dividing us, making conversations even more difficult. As our politics become more extreme, the impact on individuals also becomes more serious, affecting our physical and mental well-being.

In the first edition, Mary-Frances wrote, "Whether we like it or not, or are prepared for it or not...[p]eople are talking about these issues, or at minimum, thinking about them, and it impacts productivity, engagement, and employees' sense of safety and well-being." We would modify that for this edition to say whether we like it or not, we must be prepared to have meaningful discussions because employees are doing more than thinking about these things today, they are demanding to be heard and listened to or they will take action, including protesting and walking out the door. An estimated 50 million people quit their jobs in 2022 according to the Federal Job Openings and Labor Turnover Survey.[4] This mass exodus, dubbed the Great Resignation, saw women and people of color quit at higher rates.

Considering we have been taught not to talk about polarizing topics, especially at work, we may not know how to do it very well. Thus, our attempts may lead to counterproductive, divisive dialogue. And as our workplaces and society become more diverse, these conversations are ever-more complicated and more necessary.

Effectively engaging in Bold, Inclusive Conversations is

hard work and is getting even more difficult due to the current global, political, and social climate. Many great leaders have attempted with some success over the years to bring people across varying dimensions of difference to the table to alleviate the polarization, animosity, and hatred that has plagued humanity since the beginning of time.

We contend that the reason we are not further along—and are perhaps regressing—is because we have not approached the work in a developmental way. We have failed to fully realize and understand that not everybody who is interested is ready for Bold, Inclusive Conversations. If we were to approach the work developmentally, we would meet interested people where they are, not expect everyone to necessarily see the world from our view. We would acknowledge that while one may be learning, mistakes are inevitable. We must also realize that some people are not interested and do not want to learn. They are rooted in ideologies of hate and intolerance, and it is likely futile to attempt to engage them in Bold, Inclusive Conversations.

For those who want to develop the skills to engage in inclusive conversations, we must exercise patience. New skills take time: for example, someone learning to ride a bike will likely fall before mastering the art of peddling smoothly; someone trying to solve an advanced algebra problem before taking Algebra 101 will likely be unsuccessful and may give up. We urge everyone to cut each other some slack—be patient, encouraging, and forgiving. In his book *Outliers*, Malcolm Gladwell asserts that it takes 10,000 hours of practice to achieve mastery in any skill. And we posit that once you have achieved mastery, let's say as an accomplished pianist, you still don't stop practicing. You never stop learning new pieces. The same is true for engaging in Bold, Inclusive Conversations. Our model emphasizes the role of culture, cultural differences, and the critical nature of reflection. Closure is not the endgame.

We Can't Talk about That at Work! provides an effective guide to developing the skills necessary to engage in conversations around polarizing topics, acknowledging that these topics are complex, that there are no simple answers, and that it takes time and practice to learn how to do it well.

Keep in mind that this book is a guide and not a prescription for how to have Bold, Inclusive Conversations. There is no one right answer and no one fail-proof model. Throughout the book, we try to offer a number of considerations before you embark on a difficult conversation, as well as some examples of what may work and why other approaches may not.

We are failing to find a shared purpose that binds all of humanity together. Rather than moving more toward shared meaning and understanding, we are staying in our own corners with like-minded people, entrenched in our own ideologies, unable to find a common vision.

In this updated guide, we will support you in answering some of the same questions we addressed in the first edition with new examples, updated research, and new insights. When you have been personally impacted by some of the unfortunate events of our time, how do you maintain your level of engagement at work? How do you share your feelings and thoughts with your manager or coworkers? Is there a level of trust present to engage in topics like race, religion, and politics?

You may not personally feel that you are impacted by some of these events but empathize with coworkers who have been. How can you become an effective, supportive ally and build trust among coworkers from different walks of life? What skills are required to initiate these conversations?

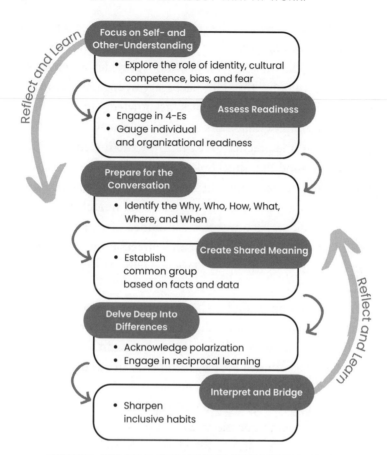

FIGURE 1. THE BOLD, INCLUSIVE CONVERSATIONS MODEL

As a leader, how do you manage employees from diverse backgrounds who have different perspectives and experiences? How do you encourage and facilitate inclusive conversations about polarizing topics so that all employees feel valued, respected, and safe?

We Can't Talk about That at Work! lays out a blueprint for developing the skills necessary to effectively engage in conversations about polarizing issues. Figure 1 (The Bold,

Inclusive Conversations Model) depicts a process for engaging in these conversations and will serve as the structure for the book. In Chapter 1, we explore the reasons why it is important to learn how to engage in Bold, Inclusive Conversations in the workplace. The subsequent chapters expound on each phase presented in this figure.

If you are interested in engaging in conversations to create a more inclusive world, this book will start you on your journey.

Yours inclusively,
Mary-Frances Winters and Mareisha N. Reese

◆ ◆ ◆

ONE

Why Do We Have to Talk about *That* at Work?

When we avoid difficult conversations, we trade
short-term discomfort for long-term dysfunction.

PETER BROMBERG

Why in the world would we want to encourage employees
to talk about polarizing topics in the workplace? We come to
work to make products and provide services for our customers, members, and/or clients—not to talk about social issues.
Topics such as race, politics, and religion are inappropriate
and should be discouraged. Perhaps this is how you feel. For
generations, this has been the prevailing sentiment for many
organizations and corporate environments. However, there
are compelling reasons why a position of avoidance is no
longer the best policy.

The most persuasive reason for building the skills necessary for Bold, Inclusive Conversations at work is that in
this ever-increasingly polarized sociopolitical climate, they
are already being talked about—a lot! Social media is a huge
factor in the increased visibility of and exposure to current issues. And most of us lack the skills to have effective
dialogue.

The goal of this book is to help you make the conversations that are already happening more productive, supportive,
and inclusive, leaving people feeling whole and ultimately

resulting in better teamwork, productivity, engagement, and overall well-being.

A POLARIZED SOCIETY LEADS TO
A POLARIZED WORKPLACE

As the workforce becomes more diverse, there are more people from different racial/ethnic groups, religious affiliations, political affiliations, generations, sexual orientations, gender identities, and **disability** statuses who may be facing very different realities than ever before. We are living in times of heightened social conflict around race, religion, and politics. The last few years have been filled with instances of police violence, mass shootings, immigration debates, reproductive rights debates, religious intolerance against Muslims and Jews, heightened attacks on the transgender community, domestic and international terrorism, and extreme political divisions, making it impossible for many not to bring strong emotions about these issues into the workplace.

Social scientists contend that the more we feel threatened, the greater our tendency to be polarized.[5] We've found that many people feel that their way of life is being threatened by terrorism, demographic shifts, and new technology. When people are fearful, the gut level response is to blame other groups for their plight. With so many complex issues facing society today, we see more polarization than ever before. We find ourselves in the throes of cultural wars on many fronts. Consider these realities:

- The murder of George Floyd in 2020 sparked new and more serious discussions about racism in this country. The Black Lives Matter movement gained strength and also intense backlash. Workplace discussions about race and racism became more commonplace, albeit not without difficulty. It is not clear that we have made significant

progress in effectively talking about race in the workplace. We continue to hear "we are not ready for that" or
"it just makes us too uncomfortable."

◆ Race-based affirmative action in higher education was
struck down by a 6–3 Supreme Court decision in 2023[6]
and soon after conservative groups began to attack
race-focused diversity, **equity**, and inclusion efforts in
the corporate world. Conservatives have weaponized the
term *woke*, meant to convey an awareness of societal
inequities. Instead, they promote an "anti-woke" agenda
where any efforts designed to correct inequities (e.g.,
transgender rights, reproductive health care rights, racial
discrimination) is deemed harmful to society. Workplace
conversations are critical to clarify and reinforce the commitment to inclusive policies and practices.

◆ Numerous mass shootings, many in schools and some in
workplaces, continue to intensify calls for more gun control, mostly to no avail. Parents fear for their children's
safety and workers fear for theirs in the workplace. This
obviously political issue has polarized the United States.
Workplace discussions are important to understand and
clarify policies and practices that ensure worker safety,
both physically and emotionally.

◆ The world was hit by a global pandemic (COVID-19) in
2020 that put us on lockdown for months, killed hundreds of thousands of people, and left others suffering
physically and emotionally as it disrupted any sense of
normalcy in almost every aspect of our lives. Even the
pandemic was fraught with extreme polarization. There
were diametrically opposed views about the utility
of wearing masks or receiving vaccines as preventive
measures. "Anti-vaxxers" engaged in sometimes violent
attacks on people wearing masks and advocating for

vaccinations. Because of the widespread belief that the virus originated in a lab in China, anti-Asian hate crimes increased 339 percent in 2021 according to the Center for the Study of Hate and Extremism.[7]

◆ The pandemic had a major impact on the workplace when in-person work moved to virtual arrangements. As the threat of the virus subsided, we saw a dramatic increase in **hybrid work** environments where workers alternated between in-person and at-home settings. These new and unfamiliar working arrangements call for new ways to effectively communicate. How can we best share feelings in a virtual space? Are **historically marginalized groups** at more of a disadvantage in virtual workspaces?

◆ Political polarization has become so severe that many of us sat shocked as we watched the 2021 takeover of the US Capitol by Donald Trump supporters who erroneously believed that the election was "stolen" by Joe Biden. We were in a team meeting at The Winters Group when the insurrection took place. It was triggering for many to watch, to the point of needing to take some time away for our emotional well-being. It also led to the need for group support and processing. We feel sure that ours was not the only workplace that needed to talk about this unprecedented and disturbing event.

◆ In 2022, **antisemitism** increased 36 percent, the highest level since 1979, with the number of antisemitic incidents rising 500 percent over the last decade.[8]

◆ When the Supreme Court overturned *Roe v. Wade* in 2022, many organizations scrambled to provide their employees with alternatives, such as paying for them to travel to abortion-friendly states.[9]

◆ A number of states have put in place anti-transgender legislation to deny gender-affirming health care and prohibit trans women and girls from participating in school sports. In 2023 49 states proposed at least 566 anti-transgender bills, and 80 passed while 128 failed.[10]

◆ A wave of so-called anti-woke bills call for banning books in schools and libraries on slavery, race, racism, and feminism as well as banning terms like critical race theory and even words like *diversity, equity,* and *inclusion* in workplace training. Since 2021, at least 44 states have introduced bills or taken other steps to restrict the teaching of what they deemed to be critical race theory.[11]

◆ Hate crimes against all **marginalized** groups have reached an all-time high, increasing by 11.6 percent in 2021 according to the FBI. Fifty-six percent of these crimes are perpetuated against Black people.[12]

◆ We are witnessing polarized views on what constitutes our First Amendment rights. What does freedom of speech mean? Will you face retribution for speaking up about issues you care about? In 2023 two Black legislators from Tennessee were expelled from the legislature for joining a protest of high school students advocating for gun control after a mass shooting at a Catholic elementary school where three students and three staff members were killed. In a call for justice, both were later reinstated.[13] These are just a few examples of why we need to develop the skills for Bold, Inclusive Conversations.

POLARIZATION THWARTS INCLUSION; INCLUSION DRIVES ENGAGEMENT

Polarization thwarts attempts for inclusion. Polarization is the opposite of inclusion. Polarization fosters an "us-and-them" environment, whereas inclusion attempts to create a sense of belonging and unity. Most major organizations today have a goal to create an inclusive culture because they realize that inclusion drives engagement. As reported in a Gallup study, inclusion and engagement are highly correlated: The most engaged employees rated their company high on diversity and inclusion. The least engaged employees rated their company very low on the questions related to diversity and inclusion.[14] The Winters Group conducted a survey with a large financial institution that showed similar results. Inclusion was the highest correlated factor for engagement. Another study conducted in 2023 by The Winters Group among twenty of our clients showed that job satisfaction was highly correlated to perceptions of racial justice in the workplace.

According to a study by Catalyst that surveyed Australian workers, employees who experienced psychological safety felt that they could freely speak up about problems and tough issues.[15] Our perception of **psychological safety** is based on a belief about the organization's norms or culture. The same study identified four leadership characteristics—accountability, courage, humility, and empowerment—that enable psychological safety across race, gender, and other demographic variables. We speak to courage and cultural humility in Chapter 2.

THE IMPACT OF SOCIAL MEDIA
ON POLARIZATION

Social media outlets exacerbate the increase in polarization. Instantaneous access to breaking news and opinions via tools such as X (formerly Twitter), Facebook, Snapchat, Instagram, and others has magnified opportunities to engage in contentious conversation and debate. People routinely use their smartphones to record all sorts of events that go viral for the whole world to see and comment on.

The proliferation of "fake news" contributes to increasing

polarization around political issues. Since the 2016 US election, we have seen an increase in how social media fuels polarization through the spread of misinformation and disinformation. Both are defined as false information; however disinformation is spread with intent to mislead or deceive people.

Disinformation has become so prevalent that more than 90 percent of journalists surveyed by the writers advocacy group PEN America[16] said they have had to change their practices, including spending more time debunking disinformation and communicating their efforts to be transparent in their reporting methods.

Before social media, we weren't as likely to be bombarded with polarizing topics such as race, religion, and politics unless we were news junkies. In the workplace, it is easy, even if against company policy, to have ongoing access to social media on our smart devices. As a result, many people constantly debate and share their opinions and beliefs on social media; and to the extent that they are virtually connected to coworkers, these conversations take place at work, or in a workplace context. Social media makes it very easy to know the beliefs and opinions of our coworkers.

The more that an individual's personal beliefs are repeated (i.e., go viral), the more they become accepted as fact. Paradoxically, the more an individual's or a group's beliefs are challenged, the more that person or group believes them. When beliefs are challenged, the human tendency is to become more obstinate and determined to defend the opinion. Any attention to the belief or opinion, positive or negative, acts as fuel for the fire.

Social media platforms can keep our emotions in high gear. We tell our social media followers and connections what we like and what we don't like. When we disagree, we continue to post more rationale for our own position, and they, in turn, post more for their position, increasing the polarization. In the extreme, when a connection posts something we don't like, we can block them. In other words, we can stay firmly rooted in our own beliefs, totally rejecting another's viewpoint. We take an "I don't want to hear it" attitude and, in some cases, an "I don't like you anymore" stance. We are often unable to separate the person from their position. We discuss the need to separate the person from the position in Chapter 3.

Many people today are addicted to social media. Social and behavioral scientists are busy studying the psychological ramifications of this phenomenon. Many people have shared with us that by disconnecting from social media they feel less stressed. Some, who have not done so, bring these intense emotions and associated anxiety with them to work. And they do not stop communicating on polarizing issues just because they are at work.

THE IMPACT ON EMPLOYEES, IN THEIR OWN WORDS

The Winters Group creates space for open dialogue for a variety of different clients, supporting them in effectively addressing the aftermath of recent traumatic events and the polarized views that seem to always come with them. The sessions open with the prompt "Describe how you are feeling in one word." The responses range from depressed, despondent, frustrated, angry, helpless, and hopeless to encouraged, energized, hopeful, and optimistic. However, the majority of the emotions are negative.

Psychologists believe that the recurrence of unfortunate events intensifies our feelings of stress and trauma. The more we see images of police shootings, terrorist attacks, and other acts of violence, the more we are likely to experience effects likened to post-traumatic stress syndrome. Individuals who are most impacted by these events—for instance, Black men fearful that they will be wrongly targeted by police, Muslim women in hijabs afraid they will be subject to bullying or worse, transgender employees afraid to use the bathroom that corresponds to their gender identity—are likely distracted at work. This impacts engagement and productivity.

The Winters Group has conducted several public, free virtual learning webinars to address some of these issues. One was called Race & Workplace Trauma during the Age of #BlackLivesMatter. More than 250 people attended. Another, called Let the Healing Begin: Restoring Our Quest for Inclusion, occurred immediately following the 2016 presidential election. Over 600 people registered for this 90-minute session. We polled participants during both sessions to explore the extent to which these events impacted their productivity at work. More than 60 percent admitted that there was either a "great deal" or "somewhat" of an impact.

Participants shared the following perspectives during these sessions:

> *"I came to work the day after the Philando Castile killing and I said to my boss that I was pretty upset, and I got nothing, not even an acknowledgment. This really shook me up and now I don't know if I can really trust her."*
> —*African American male at large consulting company*
> (We heard similar sentiments from several others from different companies.)

> *"I am Muslim, gay, and from the Middle East. That is three strikes against me. When I am waiting for the train at the metro station I don't stand near the edge because I am afraid someone might push me in. I bring that fear to work*

with me every day. It does impact my ability to concentrate and do my best work."
—male employee at a not-for-profit research organization

"I was at work and got a call from my child at school. He was terrified because the kids were telling him that he was going to be deported. I felt a need to leave and go and get him. My boss understood."
—Latine employee at a large service organization

"Our company sent out a statement after the Pulse Night Club shooting but said nothing about the killings of unarmed Black men. Why does one group deserve acknowledgment and sympathy and our group [African Americans] does not?"
—African American employee at a large consulting firm
   (We have heard similar statements from African Americans at several different companies.)

"I have not been affected by these events at all. I could not have imagined the impact that it is having on you. It is shocking to me that you are fearful based on who you are."
—white senior leader in a not-for-profit research organization

"I work from home. I am isolated. I don't know what the sentiment is at the company really. I just know that my ability to stay focused on work has been impacted. I did look for a message from leadership. I think it would have helped."
—African American woman at a large consulting firm

"One of my coworkers was literally gloating after Donald Trump won the presidential election. I don't mind showing happiness that your candidate won, but the tone was like, 'See, now you people will have to know your place again.'"
—African American woman at a government agency

"As a Muslim doctor, I have patients who ask for a different physician because they do not want to be seen by a Muslim. I have colleagues who are visiting nurses, who have doors shut in their faces when they arrive for home health care services because of the color of their skin. We have to talk about these issues in the workplace."
—Muslim doctor at a large health care organization

"I am the only person of Middle Eastern descent on my team. I overhear conversations about terrorists, but they never discuss that with me. As a matter of fact, I think they purposefully avoid such conversations around me. It makes me feel isolated. I don't really feel like I am a part of the team."
—Muslim engineer at a large technology company

However, incidences of unequal treatment that impact historically marginalized groups are certainly not new.

More than a decade ago, I (Mary-Frances) was conducting a diversity strategy session for a large insurance company in the Midwest. It was a three-day event composed of senior leaders charged with developing the company's inclusion strategy. On the second day, one of the African American male participants arrived a few minutes late, visibly distracted. Later, I learned that police had stopped him on his way to the session, which we had held at a venue in a high-income part of town. No infraction had occurred. The police officer had asked to see his license and wanted to know his destination. The officer then asked where he lived, where he worked, and what brought him to that area.

The African American executive found this incident extremely disturbing. He did not want to share the details publicly with the rest of the group, even though it was a diversity session, because his organization, in his estimation, was not ready to really deal with such issues. He admitted to me that he had difficulty continuing to engage in the session.

How many people bring similar stresses with them to work as a result of being targeted just because of what they look like? How many feel that they must suffer in silence?

COMPANY SILENCE TRANSLATES INTO "YOU DON'T CARE"

During The Winters Group's virtual learning sessions, we ask: "What is the impact when your manager and your company are silent about what is going on in the external world?" The most common response is: "We don't think they care." Employees who are impacted, either directly or indirectly, by these events are looking for their companies to say something. Organizations do not operate in a bubble; what happens in the external world has a direct impact on employees, and they talk about it at work whether we like it or not.

Additionally, we are finding that younger generations (Generation Z and millennials) expect organizations to speak out against societal issues. Deloitte's 2023 Gen Z and Millennial Survey found that the majority of millennials and Gen Zs feel their employers should take a leading role in addressing social issues ranging from inequity to environmental sustainability. In the same survey, they ranked business leaders as third among groups with the most significant role to play in addressing these issues, just after politicians and social justice and sustainability advocates.[17] Therefore, when thinking about recruitment and retention, organizations cannot remain silent toward these issues if they want to attract and keep new talent. However, after the outpouring of organizational support to escalate **antiracism** initiatives in 2020, by 2023 many organizations had ratcheted back on diversity, equity, and inclusion (DEI) initiatives. Their voices were not as loud, progress had slowed, and more DEI officers were leaving than were being hired.[18]

CEO's Story Reveals Aha Moment

AT&T's former CEO, Randall Stephenson, made a public statement at an employee meeting about Black Lives Matter. "Our communities are being destroyed by racial tension and we're too polite to talk about it," he said, referring to shootings and protests in Charlotte, North Carolina; Ferguson, Missouri; Baton Rouge, Louisiana; and Dallas, Texas.[19]

Stephenson also shared a story of his struggles with understanding the US racial divide. One of Stephenson's longtime friends, who happens to be African American, provided an aha experience for him. Stephenson said that he learned that his friend's life as an African American male doctor is fraught with being called negative names, being mistaken for the server in restaurants, and needing to always carry his ID, even in his own neighborhood, because of experiences with law enforcement.

Stephenson told his employees that he was embarrassed that he had known this man for many years, had shared intimate moments, counted him as one of his best friends, and had no idea of his daily struggles as a Black man in America. At the end of his speech, the employees cheered. In that moment, Stephenson made himself vulnerable and passionately articulated the compelling reason for having the courage to dialogue about our differences. The world now knows Stephenson's stance. The video has garnered hundreds of thousands of YouTube views. In an increasingly competitive hiring market, we think this will boost efforts to attract diverse talent to AT&T.

One Company's Proactive Approach Leads the Way

In 2020 and 2021, after the murder of George Floyd and the subsequent protests that ensued around the world, clients hired us to engage in listening sessions to better understand how BIPOC employees were affected by the events and how to support them with co-creating coping strategies. We also included sessions for aspiring allies that included the history of race and racism, and how to be a supportive ally.

For one client, a large nonprofit health care organization, The Winters Group facilitated a total of twenty-seven sessions with employees about the current racial climate. Four of the twenty-seven sessions were facilitated with only Black employees, to center the experiences and feelings of Black people within the organization while also providing a space to process the current climate, co-create coping strategies, and share their perspectives on what a reimagined workforce would look like. Open sessions with a mixed group of employees were held to introduce the history and theoretical underpinnings of racism, making the connection between the past and present day; we also covered how to be an ally.

Throughout the sessions, we gathered a few key themes from both the general and the Black employee–only dialogues regarding the current racial climate and their feelings at work.

General Dialogue: Participants expressed general feelings of sadness and discontent, but also enlightenment and a willingness to learn and educate themselves and others in personal and professional settings. People had a desire to practice allyship and actively participate in making change. They were also appreciative of their organization for offering a learning opportunity to its employees.

Black Employee Dialogue: During these dialogues, people expressed feelings of being judged and/or unsafe in bringing their racial identity to work. Many felt that their capabilities were not acknowledged and that they lacked opportunities for advancement. They desired a long-term commitment from organizational leadership for continued dialogue and education, as well as their participation in strategic decision-making related to the organization's culture and talent development.

We shared these themes and direct quotations from sessions with the organization's leadership to assist them with developing a strategic path forward to support their Black employees. Holding psychologically safe spaces for dialogue after polarizing events can help in building the capability for dialogue across difference. *Harvard Business Review* research found that only 8 percent of HR leaders said they felt their managers were prepared for conversations discussing diversity, equity, and inclusion. However, if managers have attended a listening session, town hall, or company-wide meeting on the topic in the last twelve months, Gallup data shows that managers are more than twice as likely to strongly agree that they're prepared to have DEI conversations.[20]

Virtual Learning Labs Provide Tools

A large trade association attended one of The Winters Group's public virtual sessions on race-based trauma. Following that, the organization hosted a series of what it calls Health Hints to continue to discuss the topic and provide employees with coping strategies and tips on how to be an ally. In conjunction with these efforts, they retained The Winters Group to offer a virtual learning opportunity to further enhance employees' capabilities in having Bold, Inclusive Conversations around race and trauma. The session explored the current state of race relations and implications for the workplace and provided strategies for engaging in meaningful dialogue around race. The evaluations showed that employees who attended felt better equipped to manage the stressors and to engage in effective dialogue.

ENGAGING IN CONVERSATIONS SENDS THE SIGNAL THAT AN ORGANIZATION CARES

Participants agree that just allowing the opportunity for dialogue is cathartic and sends a message that the organization is sensitive to the impact of these types of events. Most say that they just wanted to share their feelings and hear how others might be coping. However, progressive companies recognize that this initial sharing session is not enough. People may feel better for the moment, but despite heightened awareness, they lack solutions. For effective dialogue to continue, employees need the skills necessary to go deeper in fostering mutual understanding. Skill building takes time, which is why organizations conduct ongoing skill-building training for their employees. Chapters 5 and 6 focus on building and practicing these skills.

You may not be able to precisely account for the loss of productivity caused by the emotional toll of tragic events or immediately gauge the enhanced engagement that may come from employers' acknowledging the impact, but it can be significant. Taking a proactive approach demonstrates to employees that the company cares and wants to support them. It is critical to develop ways to have meaningful conversations across difference. In the end, it will help to create an environment that allows every employee to feel like they belong.

CHAPTER 1 ◆ TIPS FOR TALKING ABOUT IT!

◆ Recognize that whether we approve or not, employees talk about issues like race, religion, politics, and other polarizing topics in the workplace, and many do not have the skills to do so effectively.

◆ Because workplaces have become increasingly diverse with different racial/ethnic groups, religions, sexual orientations, and so on, we will need to pay attention to the needs of different groups in order to engage all employees.

◆ Realize that the tragic events that keep occurring in our world impact different groups in different ways and can negatively influence productivity, engagement, and employees' sense of safety.

◆ Recognize that employees bring their fears and other emotions into the workplace.

◆ Promote inclusion and provide resources to support employees in addressing their concerns.

◆ Provide tools and resources to develop skills to effectively talk about polarizing topics.

◆ Create psychologically safe spaces for Bold, Inclusive Conversations to occur. This reduces anxiety and increases workers' sense of well-being, which, in turn, enhances productivity, engagement, and inclusion.

◆ ◆ ◆

Get Yourself Ready for Bold, Inclusive Conversations

When I discover who I am, I'll be free.

RALPH ELLISON

Chapter 1 focuses on the compelling reasons for learning how to engage in Bold, Inclusive Conversations. This chapter will outline how to get ready for these conversations. As highlighted in the Introduction, this is hard work. And the hard work begins with you. The first step is self-understanding, and the next step, which we talk about in Chapter 3, is understanding those who are different from us.

A key reason for not being able to effectively dialogue about polarizing topics is our lack of cultural self-awareness. Bold, Inclusive Conversations about race, religion, politics, and other polarizing subjects require different skills than other types of conversations. Historically we have not wanted to talk about these topics because it is just too hard; it makes us uncomfortable and often elicits strong emotional responses.

We don't necessarily consider the ability to dialogue about race or other difficult topics as a real skill. Our behaviors would suggest that we think we can expect individuals from vastly different lived experiences and worldviews to sit together and discuss controversial and polarizing issues without the readiness and preparation to do so effectively.

Getting ready is a developmental process that involves learning more about yourself, assessing your current capabilities, and becoming willing to do the work to become more culturally competent. Readiness can actually take a long time because it is a skill that develops over time through knowledge acquisition and practice.

The readiness work for **dominant culture groups** that are considered the "norm" in society may be different than the readiness work for marginalized, **racialized**, and **oppressed** groups.

EXPLORE YOUR CULTURAL IDENTITY

The first step is to explore your cultural identity. Our **cultural identity** shapes our worldviews and thus the different opinions, attitudes, ideologies, and assumptions that we bring into our conversations.

> *We as humans must deal with an identity*
> *located in the core of the individual yet also*
> *in the core of our cultural community.*
>
> Erik Erikson[21]

Before you can have Bold, Inclusive Conversations, you must engage in deep introspection and self-reflection. Ask yourself: Who am I culturally? How do I identify? What aspects of my identity are important to me? What have I been socialized to believe? We can use an exercise called I Am to start the journey to self-understanding. Let us share our I Ams to model this exercise.

◆ Mareisha's I Am: *I am a Black,* **cisgender**, *able-bodied,* **heterosexual** *woman, Xennial (cusp of millennial and Generation X), Christian, wife, sister, introvert, analytical thinker, raised in upstate New York, living in the South-eastern United States.*

◆ Mary-Frances's I Am: *I am a Black, cisgender, hetero-sexual woman, baby boomer, mother, extrovert, entre-preneur, author, raised in upstate New York.*

These intersecting identities shape how we think, what we believe, our worldviews, and the lens through which we see the world. This type of self-inquiry is necessary before engaging in Bold, Inclusive Conversations because you have to be clear on who you are before you can be open to understanding who someone else is and why they might have a different worldview.

What Do We Mean by Culture?

It is important to understand what we mean by culture. **Culture** can be defined as the behavioral interpretation of how a group lives out its values to survive and thrive, or the unwritten practices, rules, and norms of a group. Most often, we take our culture for granted. It just "is." However, our culture drives our behavior. Do we believe in shaking hands, bowing, or kissing when we meet someone new? Is it okay to show your emotions, or does your cultural norm discourage emotional expressiveness when you feel passionate or even angry about something? What does assertiveness look like in your culture? Is it a positive or negative attribute? When we find ourselves out of our cultural norm, we begin to recognize our own unique cultural patterns.

If you are a member of a dominant group (e.g., white, male, heterosexual), you may not have to come out of your cultural comfort zone very often. We often hear leaders and others in training sessions struggle with an exercise that explores their cultural identity. Some say, "I don't really have a culture." While others will say, "I just never thought about it before." In the end, they find the exercise very self-revealing. Everybody has a cultural connection. There is no such thing

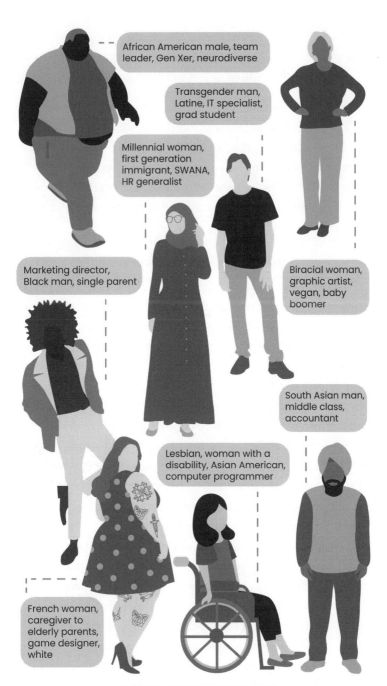

FIGURE 2. INTERSECTIONALITY

as a view from nowhere. We get our worldview from some-where, and uncovering that will enhance our cultural self-understanding. If you are a member of a group where your culture is considered the norm or dominant, you may not recognize or even accept other cultural ways of being. Believing that your own culture is the only or right way and others are wrong is what leads to polarization and the inability to engage in Bold, Inclusive Conversations. Such a belief is called **ethnocentrism**. Pause and give that some thought. To what extent are you rigid in your beliefs? Are you more judgmental than curious about other cultures?

If you are a member of a cultural group that has been marginalized or **minoritized** and subjected to ethnocentrism, your identity may play a more important role in how you see yourself and how others see you.

Culture is complex and bigger than any one of our identities. It is the combination of who we are and how we see and interpret the world—why we believe what we believe: what is good or bad, right or wrong. It includes our race/ethnicity, nationality, religion, gender, gender identity, geographic location, values and traditions, and more. Our worldview is formed from our membership in a cultural community. Figure 2 is an example of the myriad combinations of identities that one might hold. Try it: How would you complete your I Am?

These combinations are known as intersectionality.

What Is Intersectionality
and Why Is It Important to Self-Understanding?

Intersectionality is a critical concept in understanding identity and adds to the complexity of self-understanding. An example of how intersectionality manifests is reflected in the

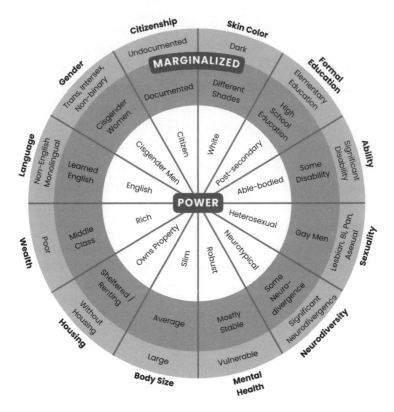

FIGURE 3. WHEEL OF POWER AND PRIVILEGE

Source: The Winters Group, Inc., adapted from ccrweb.ca by @sylviaduckworth

experiences of the gay, Muslim, Middle Eastern employee who called out his multiple identities in Chapter 1. Intersectionality theory acknowledges the overlapping and interdependent nature of simultaneously being a member of several historically marginalized groups.

First introduced by sociologist Kimberlé Crenshaw in 1989 in a critique of feminist and antiracism discourse, intersectionality challenged the effectiveness of gender and civil rights ideologies, which had traditionally excluded the unique experiences of Black women. For women of color, the compounding effects of belonging to multiple marginalized identities (e.g., Black, woman, low socioeconomic class) created a unique experience that was often overlooked in the inquiry into and development of solutions that sought to address race and gender issues. According to intersectionality, the context and degree to which we experience power or marginalization is influenced by the intersection of our varying identities.

As shown in Figure 3, those who belong to nondominant groups are usually farther away from power and more aware of their identities because they are often treated inequitably in society. The cultural exercise below encourages self-understanding. Members of historically marginalized groups tend to find the following questions easier to answer because of their often-subordinated status in society (e.g., BIPOC, LGBTQIA+, those from a non-Christian religious group). Whether you see yourself as a member of a dominant group or of one that has been historically marginalized, assess your cultural awareness.

Ask yourself:

◆ *Who am I culturally?*

Where did I grow up?

What was the culture of my community?

What did I learn about right/wrong, good/bad?

What are my values and beliefs and how have they changed over time?

How would I describe a cultural community to which I belong?

◆ *What is my cultural identity?*

Race/ethnicity

Generation

Religion

Education

Profession

Political affiliation

How does my cultural identity shape who I am and how I think?

◆ *What is my mindset about difference?*

Do I believe that we are basically all the same as humans?

That we are more alike than we are different?

That "I don't see color" or "I don't see gender"?

That people are different, but my group's cultural norms are really better?

That differences are normal, inevitable, something to learn about?

Gaining cultural self-understanding is not necessarily intuitive, especially for those in the dominant group. It takes time. Spend time with yourself understanding who you are. Seek a partner, perhaps a family member or a trusted friend who can help you on the journey.

How Is Our Worldview Limited?

We are experts of our own experiences but certainly not the lived experiences of others. When someone of another race or ethnicity says that they do not believe that racism still exists, the question to them is, How would you know? Your lived experience is very different from many others. To have Bold, Inclusive Conversations, we have to honor the diverse perspectives that come from different lived experiences.

Other examples are the assertions that "I do not see color" or "I don't see you as a Black person, just as a person." While we want to be acknowledged as human, we also want our unique identities and cultures to be acknowledged. We recognize that most people who make such statements mean well, that they are saying they see the other person as the "same as them"—we are equals. However, when people say such things, they really do see the difference or they would not have to call it out. The reality is, our racial identities are differences that matter in our society. Individuals from dominant groups who are less likely to have experienced "otherness" must acknowledge the limitations of their worldview to have Bold, Inclusive Conversations. It is important to come to conversations with cultural humility, recognizing the limitation of our own lens.

Why Is the Golden Rule Limited?

Since the passage of the **Civil Rights Act of 1964** in the United States, when it became illegal to discriminate based on race, ethnicity, nationality, gender, or religion, we have focused on treating people "the same," being "color blind" or "gender blind," and so on. (We recognize that the use of the term *blind* can be considered **ableist** language in this context.) The legislation says that we should treat people equally. In our minds, equal might translate to "the same." Many strive to practice the golden rule (treating others the way you want to be treated), rather than the **platinum rule** (treating others the way they want to be treated). You will not know how others want to be treated unless you have some level of understanding about them. Operating from the assumption that you know what is good for others because you know what is good for you can thwart efforts for mutual understanding.

The golden rule is a good starting point, but Bold, Inclusive

Conversations are much more effective if you have the capability to practice the platinum rule. If we assume that we are basically all the same and minimize our differences, we have no incentive to spend time learning about others from a different race, sexual orientation, ethnicity, and so on because we feel we have essentially nothing to learn. A dominant group individual will more likely enter a conversation with the underlying assumption of "sameness." While it is important to start a conversation with the goal of reaching common ground—what we have in common—it is also important not to minimize or deny differences in perspective based on cultural identity. We will discuss the concept of minimization in more detail later in this chapter.

How Do We Achieve Common Ground?

We have to find some commonality to have a Bold, Inclusive Conversation, which we talk about in detail in Chapter 3. A "sameness" mindset can be a good place to start when we encounter polarized views. You want to find the common ground, a place of agreement from which to start the conversation. For example, some agreements might include: we all want our communities to be safe; we all want the best for our children. However, we may have different worldviews of how to accomplish these goals. Discovering our commonalities builds trust and an opening for deeper dialogue.

In polarized situations, the human tendency is to judge the other's perspective as wrong. We become so entrenched in our own beliefs that we retreat to our own corners, rather than to a place of nonjudgmental curiosity about why we have different views. For example, white people may be more likely to hold the worldview that police officers are our "friends." Based on experience, Black communities in particular, may have learned the exact opposite. To have Bold, Inclusive Conversations we have to explore our similarities (e.g., we all want our communities to be safe) before we can effectively talk about our different perspectives based on our different lived experiences. To be able to engage in such exploration, we have to continue to grow in self-awareness by asking Why do I believe that? Why do others believe something so different? That curiosity can lead to a fruitful dialogue, which we explore later in the book.

Do We Just "Go Along to Get Along"?

Often, individuals from historically marginalized groups minimize their differences, or take a "go along to get along" stance, as a means of survival in dominant group spaces, which, in effect, can validate the "we are all the same" world-view. People with visible differences from dominant groups may find that to be accepted they have to accentuate their similarities and downplay their differences. Racial, ethnic, and other differences may make dominant group members uncomfortable. Later in the chapter, we address the issue of discomfort. This dynamic makes it even more difficult to engage in meaningful conversations. Dominant group members may over-assume similarities, and minoritized groups might feel a need to understate differences. These two dynamics void each other out and result in no progress in cross-cultural understanding and thus no effective dialogue.

Bold, Inclusive Conversations can only happen with an openness to acknowledge and address that we have differences that make a profound difference in perceptions and outcomes for many of us.

Are We Hindered by Stereotype Threats or Internalized Oppression?

Stereotype threats and internalized oppression sometimes experienced by marginalized groups may also thwart attempts at Bold, Inclusive Conversations. They may be associated with the desire on the part of marginalized groups to go along to get along. A stereotype threat, a term coined by researchers Claude Steele and Joshua Aronson, is the expectation or the fear that you will be judged based on a negative stereotype about your social identity group, rather than actual performance and potential.

Stereotype threats have been proven to have an immediate impact on performance. One study on stereotype threats and women's performance in math found that women are more likely to perform as well on math tests as men when the test is described as not producing gender differences in performance. This condition countered the stereotype that women do not do as well in math as men.

Similar results were found among African American students on standardized tests. Steele and Aronson's study found that African American students were less likely to perform well on tests described as diagnostic of intellectual ability. Even if the test was not an ability-diagnostic, Black students underperformed due to their fears of colluding with stereotypes that suggest Blacks are intellectually inferior. They overperformed when the test was described as nondiagnostic.

Although numerous lab studies in academic settings show the impact of stereotype threats on performance, the influence in work settings has not been explored very much.

In a paper in *The Counseling Psychologist*, Caryn J. Block, Sandy M. Koch, et al. explore the impact of stereotype threats at work. They contend that an individual in the minority in a workplace has a greater likelihood of experiencing stereotype threats.[22] They posit three potential responses to stereotype threats in the workplace:

♦ Fending off the stereotype threat by overcompensating. Individuals work hard to prove that the stereotype does not apply to them or that they are not a typical member of their group. They may distance themselves from the negatively stereotyped group and assimilate by trying to behave and act like a more positively viewed group. This is akin to minimizing their differences, the "go along to get along" phenomena.

◆ Becoming discouraged by the stereotype threat, which leads to disengagement because the individual believes that no matter how hard they try, the stereotype is just too big to overcome. This can manifest in disengagement from negative evaluations about their group in order to preserve self-esteem. For example, from a psychological perspective, the individual discounts negative performance evaluations and finds them not relevant to their self-perception. In the short term, disengagement may work in preserving an individual's self-esteem, but in the long term it may negatively impact motivation and performance because they believe they have no control over the outcomes.

◆ Finding resiliency to the stereotype threat. The authors believe many underrepresented groups actually manage to have this response in the workplace. It may play out in an advocacy or champion role, supporting learning and training in the organization to alleviate stereotypes; it may take the form of pointing out positive attributes of the targeted identity group or collective action, such as affinity groups that work to support inclusive practices.

A similar and more insidious concept is known as internalized oppression, where the marginalized group begins to believe the negative stereotypes about their group. With stereotype threats, the individual becomes apprehensive about confirming stereotypes about their group and tries, with behavior modification, to respond to them. With internalized oppression, the individual believes the stereotypes as truth. This belief may not be conscious, but it plays out in behaviors.

Historically marginalized groups should raise their self-awareness about stereotype threats and internalized oppression. Are one or both of these phenomena operating and inhibiting your ability to engage authentically in Bold, Inclusive Conversations? Do you hold back because you do not want to confirm a stereotype or, with internalized oppression, do you come to the conversation from a belief of inferiority? Bold, Inclusive Conversations will not be effective when the historically marginalized in the conversation have not come to full self-actualization and wholeness. If you know that you are still grappling with self-acceptance due to the impact of living in a racialized world where your identity group faces systemic "isms," you may not be ready for Bold, Inclusive Conversations. If you know that you are dealing with racial trauma, you may want to protect your well-being and refrain from conversations that may be retraumatizing. Even when someone from a marginalized group feels fully actualized, whole, and affirmed, they may still want to protect their peace by not engaging in conversations that may retraumatize. It is important for marginalized groups to set boundaries on how, how much, with whom, and when to have identity-based conversations. We discuss setting boundaries again in Chapters 5 and 6.

How Do We Experience Difference?

A useful model for understanding how we experience cultural differences is the **Intercultural Development Continuum**, assessed by the Intercultural Development Inventory (IDI) and developed and owned by Dr. Mitchell Hammer, founder of IDI, LLC.

The theory is that as our experience with difference expands, we have a greater capacity to understand and bridge

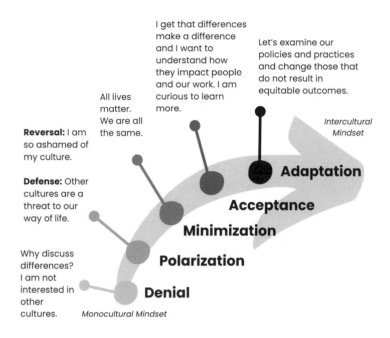

FIGURE 4. THE INTERCULTURAL DEVELOPMENT CONTINUUM

Source: The Winters Group, Inc., adapted from the
Developmental Model of Intercultural Sensitivity (DMIS)

the complexities of cultural differences. This developmental model contends that we advance through stages of greater capability to meaningfully address differences. Figure 4 highlights the developmental stages.

If we have had no experience with difference, we might be at the first stage, **denial**, where we would avoid or be disinterested in differences; the next stage is **polarization**, where we judge differences. Both denial and polarization are early developmental phases where we have little experience or knowledge of differences and can see difference only through our own cultural lens (i.e., our **ethnocentric worldview**). At polarization, the goal should be to move to minimization.

According to the theory, we must move through each stage as we develop cultural competence.

The third stage, **minimization**, is where we practice the golden rule. Here, we take the mindset that we are essentially all the same and see any differences as inconsequential because we are all human. Minimization is where most people fall on the continuum because we have essentially been taught to minimize differences. As mentioned above, historically marginalized groups often minimize their differences to "go along to get along." Individuals from dominant group identities minimize when they do not have a deeper comprehension of differences. Minimization can be a good place to find common ground to start Bold, Inclusive Conversations, but we have to go further for effective cross-cultural dialogue.

The two stages that reflect a much deeper understanding of difference—a recognition that there are differences that make a difference and the need to understand and bridge those differences—are acceptance and adaptation (**ethnorelative** stages). At these stages, we embody a more complex way of experiencing difference and can view the world from the perspective of other cultures. **Acceptance** does not mean agreement. It means that we accept that there are a number of different ways that cultures experience the world and are curious to learn more about our differences. At **adaptation**, not only do we recognize patterns of differences in our own and other cultures but we also know how to effectively bridge those differences in mutually respectful ways. The Intercultural Development Inventory (IDI), a fifty-question online psychometric inventory, can effectively provide a baseline of your individual (or group's) cultural competence, enhancing your self-understanding and, ultimately, gauging your readiness for Bold, Inclusive Conversations.[23]

How Do We Face Our Fears and Choose Courage?

We always have some level of fear when we delve into unknown territory. Bold, Inclusive Conversations require venturing outside of our comfort zone, which can be intimidating. The role of cultural identity makes dialogue even more complicated because our identity groups are linked to a broader historical and social context. Sometimes history is uncomfortable and traumatic, which can make some of us fearful of having these discussions and more inclined to want to forget (or even deny) the past. We see this in the increased efforts in many states to ban discussions about race and the history of racism. The fear on the part of those in power seems to be motivated by scarcity and a zero-sum mentality, explicitly the fear of losing power. Talking about marginalized communities might lead to action to correct inequities, and the assumption is that the dominant group would lose something. If in the United States we truly believe in liberty and justice for all, we must talk about these issues. Incidents of antisemitism, Islamophobia, racism, homophobia, and xenophobia continue to escalate and divide, polarize, and lead to violence and senseless killings. Instead of avoiding these conversations, we must identify strategies that alleviate our fears and position us to effectively engage in Bold, Inclusive Conversations. If we do not or are not allowed to have open dialogue about issues that threaten the safety of us all, our sense of civility and human decency will continue to devolve. Unfortunately, not everyone is interested in achieving equity and inclusion and therefore are not good candidates for Bold, Inclusive Conversations. Those with extreme views, who advocate for harm against those who are different from them in some aspect of their identity, are not the target audience for the recommendations in this book.

Let's pause here. You have probably chosen this book

because you care about these issues, and you want to learn how to support diversity, inclusion, and equity efforts in your professional and/or personal life. Be honest: Do you experience a sense of fear when attempting to engage in Bold, Inclusive Conversations? If so, ask yourself: What am I afraid of? These questions are relevant whether you are a member of a dominant or nondominant group. Are you afraid of:

♦ Offending?

♦ Not knowing enough about the subject?

♦ Creating conflict?

♦ Remembering some negative outcome from a previous dialogue?

♦ Being judged?

♦ Dealing with "them," who don't "get it"?

♦ Becoming triggered and reacting in a way that you might regret later?

♦ Being retraumatized?

♦ Being stigmatized?

As part of your self-discovery process, really probe why you might fear having a Bold, Inclusive Conversation. Try to lean into your discomfort. Most things that are hard create some level of discomfort. By the same token, facing the difficulty and working through it brings satisfaction in the end. We, in our work at The Winters Group, have experience with a number of people who say they want to advance in their cultural competence but then push back when the conversation becomes uncomfortable for them. And some of our clients discontinue the conversations because "They make our leaders uncomfortable." If we continue to do this, we surely will not make progress

It takes courage to face our fears. A 2022 *Forbes* article highlights seven attributes of the courageous: (1) intentionality, (2) purpose, (3) curiosity and openness, (4) commitment, (5) embracing risk, (6) adaptability, and (7) acceptance. Practice finding your courage to have Bold, Inclusive Conversations.

> *It takes courage…to endure the sharp pains of self-discovery rather than choose to take the dull pain of unconsciousness that would last the rest of our lives.*
>
> Marianne Williamson[24]

Along with courage, we need cultural humility to engage in conversations across differences. An article in the *Journal of Health Care for the Poor and Underserved* describes cultural competence in clinical training as a detached mastery of a theoretically finite body of knowledge. Cultural humility, on the other hand, incorporates lifelong commitment to self-evaluation and self-critique, to redress the power imbalances in the patient–physician dynamic. **Cultural humility** is the ability to maintain an interpersonal stance that is other-oriented (or open to the other) in relation to aspects of cultural identity that the other person deems most important.

How Do We Face Our Biases?

We all have biases, but most of us are unaware of how they manifest in our decisions and interactions. Social scientists assert that most of our biases are unconscious and that our unconscious biases drive 99 percent of our behaviors. **Unconscious bias** is a bias that happens automatically and is triggered by our brain making quick judgments and assessments of people and situations, influenced by our background, cultural environment, and personal experiences. How can you address your unconscious biases if you are unaware of them?

Know Your Culture: Increase self-understanding as discussed earlier. Know your own culture, why you believe what you believe, your history and early experiences that have shaped your value system.

Change, Expand Your Story: If you build up unconscious biases over time by ingesting biased, partial, and negative messages, then you need to work to meet those messages with positive, affirming, counter-narratives that are equally powerful in order to undo them. Counter-narratives are only possible when you know what they are. If you don't know other stories, you cannot change the one in your head.

Nigerian novelist Chimamanda Ngozi Adichie, in a compelling TED Talk called "The Danger of a Single Story," cautions that if we hear only a single story about another person or country, we risk stereotyping and vastly misinterpreting. In her talk, she says if the single story of Africa is that it is an undeveloped, poverty-ridden continent, you miss the other stories like hers—growing up in a middle-class household with college professor parents—or the rich history of a place like Timbuktu, the home of the first university in the world. What stories do you have about individuals, groups, cultures that are different from you? Is it a single story or do you have several narratives in your mind, some perhaps good, others not so good, but balanced?

The DNA model supports us in being more intentional in naming and challenging our biases.

D: Describe. First describe the behaviors and actions you see. Be careful not to let your personal judgments influence what you observe.

N: Navigate your understanding. Be aware that you have culturally influenced interpretations of the behaviors on the part of another culture. What are alternative interpretations?

A: Adapt or Act. Once you feel you have a pretty good understanding of the behaviors and actions you observed, begin to think of ways to navigate the situation effectively using mutual adaptation skills.

Let's consider this example: You see a Black man running out of a department store clutching a package. How might you interpret this behavior? Is he shoplifting? What is an alternative interpretation? Perhaps he just received word that his wife is in labor, and he needs to get to the hospital and is clutching his package so he does not drop it. How might you adapt or act? Reflect on your biases using the framework in Figure 5.

The DNA model is useful in helping us to see beyond the single story. It helps us to expand our lens.

How Do We Acknowledge Our Power and Privilege?

Power and privilege determine who sits at the table, who has access, and who can make decisions. Power also refers to the ability of individuals or groups to induce or influence systems, and the beliefs or actions of other persons or groups. Our level of power or access to power is largely dependent on our social status and group membership (e.g., membership in various social categorizations including race, class, sexual orientation, gender identity/expression, age, religion, nationality, immigrant status, ability, size, etc.). The Wheel of Power and Privilege (Figure 3), shared earlier in this chapter, provides some examples of social group power.

Privilege, at its essence, refers to the advantages that people benefit from based solely on their social status, which is

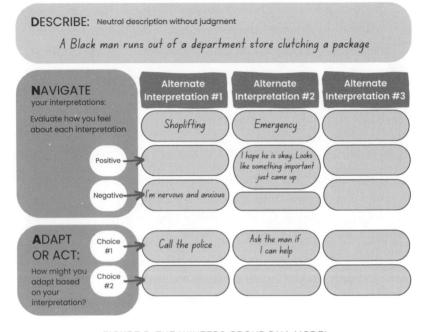

FIGURE 5. THE WINTERS GROUP DNA MODEL
Source: The Winters Group, Inc.,
adapted from D.I.E. by B. Kappler and K. Nokken

conferred by society and perpetuated by systems that favor certain groups. This status is not necessarily asked for or appropriated by individuals, which is why it can be difficult for people to see their own privilege.

Power and privilege are relative. We all have it to a certain extent in different aspects of our identity. Refer to the Wheel of Power and Privilege and assess where you have privilege. A woman or someone who identifies as non-binary might have socioeconomic privilege but not social privilege. Or remember the story in Chapter 1, the Black man stopped by police as he traveled to a work session. He may have had educational privilege, but he was disadvantaged by his race.

From a systemic view, dominant groups in society have benefited the most from unearned power and privilege. As you think about Bold, Inclusive Conversations regardless of whether you belong to the dominant or a marginalized group, consider your power and privilege.

Power and privilege are systemic and complex. Power does not have to be a zero-sum game. It can mean shared power. We can see it as infinite. In her book *The Sum of Us: What Racism Costs Everyone and How We Can Prosper Together*, author Heather McGhee, chair of the online racial justice group Color of Change, contends that policies based on a zero-sum mentality end up hurting everyone in the end.[25] A finite perspective of power leads to a defensive stance that uses deception and secrecy as the preferred strategies. When we think of power as infinite, it evokes cooperation and openness. Bold, Inclusive Conversations only happen with an infinite power worldview.

Dominant group individuals should work on understanding the impact of their unearned power and privilege. Power imbalances make Bold, Inclusive Conversations even more difficult. This work involves self-understanding and critique, cultural humility, curiosity over judgment, and a willingness to redistribute power. Historically marginalized groups must be aware of their agency in Bold, Inclusive Conversations. We are not powerless. We must find the courage to speak authentically to our truths.

Here are some general questions that you should ask yourself about power and privilege, as part of your readiness to have a Bold, Inclusive Conversation:

- What is my positional power in this situation?
- Do I have power simply because I am a member of a dominant group?
- What influence do I have over the outcomes?

◆ As a member of a marginalized group, what agency do I have in this situation?

◆ Do I see power as finite or infinite?

◆ Can I essentially live being unaware on a day-to-day basis of my identity group (e.g., race, gender, sexual orientation, immigrant status, etc.)? If so, how does this privilege impact how I show up in Bold, Inclusive Conversations?

◆ Is it likely that I will be ostracized by my friends and family because of my sexual orientation?

◆ Can I demonstrate my religious beliefs without fear?

CHAPTER 2 ◆ TIPS FOR TALKING ABOUT IT!

◆ The ability to engage in Bold, Inclusive Conversations is a journey that requires cultural self-understanding, addressing our biases and fears, and understanding our power and privilege.

◆ Know your culture. Everybody has a cultural identity that shapes their worldview. We don't always consciously realize how our culture informs our perceptions and behavior.

◆ Resist the tendency to minimize differences. We tend to minimize our differences and overstate our similarities, leading us to practice the golden rule rather than the platinum rule.

◆ Resist the single story. Many of us only have a "single story" about those who are different. Meaningful dialogue will only occur if we learn more than one story about others.

◆ Take the Intercultural Development Inventory. The IDI is a useful tool for assessing our readiness for Bold, Inclusive Conversations.

- ◆ **Recognize your power and privilege. Power and privilege are key determinants in the nature and tenor of cross-difference dialogue.**

- ◆ **Know your level of readiness before you engage in Bold, Inclusive Conversations.**

THREE

◆ ◆ ◆

Expand Your Understanding of Others and Assess Organizational Readiness

Invite people into your life who don't look like you, don't think like you, don't act like you, don't come from where you come from, and you might find that they will challenge your assumptions and make you grow as a person.

MELLODY HOBSON

The work to get ready for Bold, Inclusive Conversations starts with individual readiness; it also requires assessing organizational readiness. Chapter 2 focused on the self-understanding aspect of readiness. This chapter highlights the importance of learning about other cultures as well as assessing organizational readiness.

In her TED Talk "Color Blind or Color Brave?" Mellody Hobson, president of Ariel Capital, challenges us to venture outside our comfort zones, be intentional in engaging with our "others," and leverage difference, not only for the greater good but also for maximum business impact.[26] Let's explore why having a greater understanding of other cultures or being "color brave" is so critical to engaging in Bold, Inclusive Conversations.

WE DON'T KNOW EACH OTHER

Historically we have not had much practice interacting across differences. In some cases, there were legal restrictions that prohibited cross-cultural interactions. For example, segregation laws kept Black and white people from intermingling. Likewise, members of the LGBTQIA+ community were forced to suppress that aspect of their identity until the last several decades. Historically, our norm has been not to express political views, and many of us were taught that religious beliefs that differed from our own were "wrong."

Readiness requires a level of knowledge about differences that goes beyond your worldview. It means that you have done some study on the issues; you have listened to different perspectives, even those contrary to your own, to give you a more balanced view. As mentioned in Chapter 1, social media gives us the ability to broaden and diversify our networks. However, we typically connect only with those who are most like us. Learning to engage in meaningful dialogue across differences requires not only understanding your view but also understanding what others believe and why. This is sometimes referred to as being able to walk in another's shoes, or empathy. Many of us have only a single story about those who are different from us, as discussed in Chapter 2. We lack a wider worldview than what we get from those closest to us. We may fear learning more because we have been taught not to talk about race, politics, and other issues, especially in the workplace. The Public Religion Research Institute (PRRI) conducts studies on race and ethnicity, and one of their questions pertains to the composition of social networks by race (Figure 6). While their findings show that from 2013 to 2022, diversity has increased among social networks, white people in particular continue to respond that their networks are exclusively

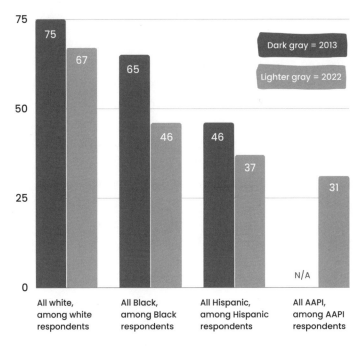

Percent of friendship network that identifies entirely as:

Dark gray = 2013

Lighter gray = 2022

FIGURE 6. RACIAL HOMOGENEITY OF FRIENDSHIP NETWORKS
Source: The Winters Group, Inc.,
adapted from Public Religion Research Institute

white (75 percent in 2013 versus 67 percent in 2022). By contrast, Black respondents improved almost 20 percentage points from 2013, where 65 percent of their networks were all Black, to 2022, when that percentage dropped to 46 percent. Latine respondents are also more likely to report a racially mixed network today than they did in 2013. Thirty-seven percent of Latines report that their social networks are composed entirely of other people who also identify as Latine, compared to 46 percent in 2013. Asian Americans and Pacific Islanders were not included in the 2013 study. In 2022, 31 percent responded that they had homogenous networks.[27]

In another survey conducted by PRRI in 2021, 50 percent of Americans believe that Muslim values are at odds with American values.[28] However, 53 percent of respondents in a 2021 Pew Research Center survey said that they do not know anyone who is a Muslim, and 52 percent said they know little or nothing at all about Islam.[29]

Integration is based on the premise that there are advantages to cross-cultural interactions. If we get to know each other better through more exposure and experience with each other, as the 4-E model recommends (see the next section), we break down the barriers and can more effectively explore our similarities and differences.

PRACTICE THE 4-Es

A critical aspect of being ready to have Bold, Inclusive Conversations about polarizing subjects is to have some knowledge of those who come from different cultural communities than your own. For this to happen, we offer the 4-Es—**exposure, experience, education,** and **empathy.**

1. Exposure

An impactful exercise called Who's in My World? invites participants to consider their own identity and the identity of those with whom they most often associate. For example, if you identify as Black, and most of the people in your world are also Black (e.g., people who regularly visit your home, people you socialize with, characters in the movies you see and books you read, close friends, people in your faith community), you are getting very little opportunity for exposure to difference. If we don't have cross-group exposure,

EXERCISE 1. WHO'S IN MY WORLD?

Complete each fill-in-the-blank using any of the following options that apply: of African descent, of Latin American descent, of Asian descent (including Indian subcontinent), of European descent, LGBTQIA+, traditionalist/silent generation, baby boomer, Generation X, millennial, Generation Z, other.

In my environment:

My coworkers are mostly

_____

My coworkers at previous jobs were mostly

_____

My supervisor is

_____

My elementary school was predominantly

_____

My high school was predominantly

_____

My teachers were mostly

_____

Most of my close friends are mostly

_____

My dentist is

_____

My doctor is

_____

People who live in my home are

_____

People who regularly visit my home are

_____

People whose homes I regularly visit are

_____

My company's customers are predominantly

_____

Roommates I've had were mostly

_____

Books I've read are written by

_____

Plays/movies I see usually have actors/themes that are

_____

Art in my home/office are by artists/themes that are mostly

_____

Friends with whom I socialize with outside of work are mostly

_____

My faith-based community is primarily

_____

the likelihood of expanding our understanding of others is limited. Who's in your world? Complete the assessment in Who's in My World (Exercise 1).

2. Experience

Experience with difference is not the same as exposure. Diversity can be all around you without you ever really creating meaningful relationships and mutual understanding. Experience is about engaging with those who are different from you in ways that are cross-culturally enriching. Forging such relationships means that you are willing to address your fears, be vulnerable, and shed single-story narratives.

Former AT&T CEO Randall Stephenson's story about his lack of knowledge of his Black friend's life experiences, discussed in Chapter 1, is a poignant example of how we can have exposure to difference without gaining meaningful experience. Developing cross-cultural relationships takes time, energy, and desire.

It may be more difficult for employees who think they have little in common to develop meaningful relationships. For instance, let's say the manager is a white male and the employee is a Southeast Asian woman. Finding commonalities to begin to connect and develop a meaningful work relationship that demonstrates that the manager cares about the employee as a person—and not just a production unit—may not be easy for either party. However, it is critical to engagement and retention, and vital in preparing for Bold, Inclusive Conversations. Sharing meaningful experiences might include external team-building events, a work-organized book club that encourages different perspectives on the content, or time in team meetings for members to talk about their culture.

One of the key drivers of engagement, according to Gallup's

Q12 Employee Engagement Survey, is that a supervisor or someone at work "seems to care about me as a person."[30] Gallup further asserts that it is important for employees to have a sense of belonging, which means feeling included. "Vaulting the Color Bar: How Sponsorship Levers Multicultural Professionals into Leadership," a study conducted by the Center for Talent Innovation, now known as Coqual, showed that 40 percent of African Americans and one-third of people of color overall feel like "outsiders" in their corporate culture, versus 26 percent of white employees who feel that way.[31] Bold, Inclusive Conversations will only be successful if employees feel that they belong, that they are cared about, and that their voices will be heard.

Encourage Reciprocal Learning

If you didn't grow up like I did then you don't know, and
if you don't know it's probably better you don't judge.

Junot Díaz[32]

The need to expand our knowledge about the other is mutual. The Winters Group offers a program called Cross-Cultural Learning Partners, which aims to foster **reciprocal learning**. We pair individuals who are different in some way (e.g., race, gender, sexual orientation, religion) and invite them to go on a guided journey of learning about each other. This includes short lessons with reflective questions and recommendations for experiences that they can share (e.g., engaging with each other's faith community or visiting a cultural museum together).

The Cross-Cultural Learning Partners program is grounded in the reciprocal nature of the learning, unlike many one-way mentoring programs, such as reverse mentoring, a very popular concept in today's workplace. **Reverse mentoring** programs are designed so that the person who is a member of the dominant group identity can learn more about the individual who is part of the nondominant group. One-way programs perpetuate an "us-and-them" environment and can contribute to polarization. Cross-cultural learning is specifically designed so that both parties are learning from each other, reducing the feeling that it is one-sided. We prefer to advocate for **reciprocal mentoring.**

Historically marginalized groups need to learn about the dominant groups as much as the dominant groups need to learn about marginalized groups. However, we contend that the historically marginalized groups may have a head start on this journey because our exposure, experience, and education has largely been from the dominant group perspective.

3. Education

Enhancing your exposure and experience is part of your education. However, those two Es need to be augmented with more formal education around differences. This can happen via workplace training, advanced university courses, movies, documentaries, museum visits, books, travel, and so on.

Beware of media reports as the only source of education about differences. We know that most reporting is biased, but beyond that, it may not provide a contextual understanding of the facts. Again, there is a danger in a single story.

The Race Forward Center for Racial Justice Innovation (now known as Race Forward) compiled a report called the Race Reporting Guide. Geared toward helping journalists, the guide asserts that most race reporting focuses on individual, specific incidents or events and fails to include a broader context, such as the role of history, institutional policies, and inequitable practices; and it rarely features much coverage of racial justice advocacy or solutions. The report calls for a more systemic analysis that looks at root causes and the mechanisms that feed into patterns.[33]

The report also asserts that language matters. The words we use can be triggers (see Chapter 8 for examples of triggers) or paint stereotypical pictures. For example, terms like *illegal immigrants* are inappropriate. *Illegal* should be used to describe an action and not the person. Understanding both the role of language and the significance of educating ourselves on broader contexts are critical to preparing for Bold, Inclusive Conversations.

Punishment without Dialogue and Learning Is Fruitless

In the age of **cancel culture**, there is a tendency to want to punish people, especially public figures, when they say something that offends a particular group. This results in a lot of media coverage and calls for their resignations, or worse; and when the action is taken against this obviously "bad" (racist/sexist/homophobic) person, we all feel better again. But what have we learned?

For those who may understand the reasons why their comments were inappropriate or offensive, punishment is often warranted. For those who may not understand the context, it may have the effect of shutting down the possibility of conversations on polarizing topics. The fear of offending or not knowing enough can loom large in these situations, and unless people choose to dig deeper and do their own learning, they may alienate themselves from that group.

In 2022, John Demsey, a senior executive at Estée Lauder, was forced to retire because of a repost on Instagram that was considered racist. Demsey said that he was careless and had not read it. He apologized immediately.[34] In a memo, Estée Lauder revealed Demsey would retire effective immediately: "This decision is the result of his recent Instagram posts, which do not reflect the values of The Estée Lauder Companies, have caused widespread offense, are damaging to our efforts to drive inclusivity both inside and outside our walls, and do not reflect the judgment we expect of our leaders."[35] The meme, which was deleted, showed Sesame Street characters wearing masks, a reference to the rapper Chingy, and the N-word. Chingy posted that he was not offended and took it that Demsey was trying to be "hip" like the kids today and it came out the wrong way.[36]

Demsey had been considered a diversity and inclusion advocate at Estée Lauder. For example, the rapper Saweetie became part of the 2022 MAC Cosmetics campaign thanks to his work. He publicly championed Grace Jones as a style icon. He raised half a billion dollars toward ending AIDS through MAC's Viva Glam campaign.[37] He did a lot of work in his more than thirty years in the beauty business to elevate Black women and also partnered with Rihanna, Mary J. Blige, and RuPaul.[38] On his popular Instagram feed, where the offense took place, he regularly posted photos of diverse beauty, in addition to other Sesame Street memes.

Demsey should definitely have taken accountability for this mistake. However, did it warrant forced retirement? And what did we learn from it? One lesson is to make sure you review and understand what you are posting. There were larger lessons missed, though, such as the cultural appropriateness of adopting terms (e.g., the N-word) only meant for people who are part of that group. Did forced retirement take care of the situation—no additional discussion needed?

Whoopi Goldberg was suspended from *The View* for two weeks in 2022 after multiple public apologies for claiming the Holocaust was not about race. She said, "It's not about race. It's about man's inhumanity to man."[39] Kimberly Godwin, president at ABC News, said she wanted the entire team to be held accountable for their words and actions. Godwin said Goldberg's actions were not aligned with those values and asked Whoopi to reflect on the impact of her comments for two weeks, adding, "ABC News...stands in solidarity with our Jewish colleagues, friends, family, and communities."[40] Goldberg invited Jonathan Greenblatt from the Anti-Defamation League on *The View* to have an educational discussion about the issue. This seems like a better solution than what happened in John Demsey's case. There was punishment, accountability, *and* education.

Public figures need to be held accountable as they have a great deal of influence. But perhaps we miss the learning opportunities when we take swift action without discussion. In Demsey's case Chingy wasn't offended. Others were. Let's talk about why. There are many other stories of public figures and others being punished for diversity faux pas. In Goldberg's case there was opportunity for education. If we are not willing to acknowledge mistakes, take accountability, forgive, and learn when the intent is good, we hinder the opportunity for Bold, Inclusive Conversations.

There are certainly boundaries. Certain comments or actions deserve consequences (i.e., punishment). Many organizations have zero-tolerance rules that they explicitly spell out in their human resources policies. We are not talking about those obvious, egregious comments that are mostly known to employees (e.g., racist, sexist, homophobic jokes; use of the N-word). We mean the type of remarks that come from the I-don't-know-what-I-don't-know place on the learning curve. For example, it might be offensive if someone asks a Black woman, "How did you get your hair like that?" or "May I touch your hair?" Rather than take offense, the Black woman can use the question as a learning opportunity to share with the person why such questions are offensive and inappropriate. If she assumes positive intent, the conversation can become very different. On the other hand, marginalized people at an individual level may be tired of teaching dominant group individuals about inappropriate comments or behavior. It can be harmful to the marginalized individual and the conversation may need to be one that encourages the dominant person to apologize and engage in their own learning.

While we must cut each other some slack for Bold, Inclusive Conversations to occur, we must also be held accountable for harmful behaviors.

Ask yourself:

◆ Do I know the history of the other group from their perspective?

◆ Do I understand the underlying systems that impact outcomes for the group(s)?

◆ What do I know in general about cultural differences (e.g., direct vs. indirect communication styles, individualistic vs. group-oriented cultures, how power is displayed, etc.)?

◆ What do I know about their values and beliefs and how and why they were shaped as they are (e.g., millennials' experience with technology differs from that of baby boomers, which shapes their worldview)?

4. Empathy

Effective dialogue across difference will not happen if we cannot be empathetic. Empathy is not sympathy. Sympathy engenders pity. Empathy leads to mutual understanding and respect. It is encompassed in the theories of emotional intelligence, a concept that is now understood to drive personal and business success. Emotional intelligence is composed of four parts: self-awareness, self-management, other awareness,

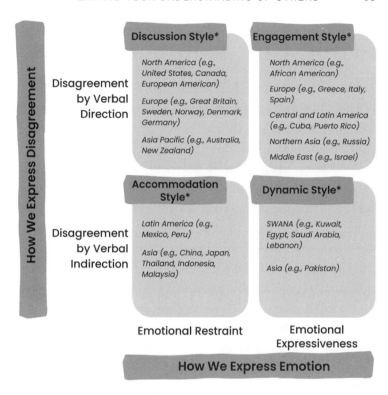

*African cultural patterns are found in the engagement, accommodation, and dynamic styles. However, some African culture groups are more discussion style depending on the influence of colonization.

FIGURE 7. INTERCULTURAL CONFLICT STYLE INVENTORY

Source: The Winters Group, Inc.,
adapted from *The Intercultural Conflict Style Model*, by M. R. Hammer

and managing relationships. Emotional intelligence is a vital ingredient for effective Bold, Inclusive Conversations.

RECOGNIZE CULTURALLY LEARNED COMMUNICATION STYLES

While there are many cross-cultural differences that have been well researched and documented, the one that is most important to understand when having Bold, Inclusive

Conversations is how we have learned to communicate and handle conflict.

The **Intercultural Conflict Style Inventory**, developed by Dr. Mitchell Hammer, helps us to distinguish cultural preferences for solving problems and handling conflict. There are four preferred styles: discussion, engagement, accommodation, and dynamic, as shown in Figure 7.

Discussion style is most preferred by Euro-American, Northern European, and Canadian cultures. It is characterized as direct and emotionally controlled. **Engagement style** is most commonly found among African Americans, Greeks, some Western Europeans, and some Latine cultures. Engagement style is direct and emotionally expressive. **Accommodation style,** preferred by many Asian cultures, is indirect and emotionally restrained. **Dynamic style**, common among Middle Eastern cultures, is indirect and emotionally expressive.[41]

Those who prefer discussion style will advocate for logical, rational, fact-based arguments with limited emotional expressiveness, while those whose style is either dynamic or engagement-oriented will be comfortable with a strong display of emotion; they may be more apt to tell stories or use metaphors and circular reasoning. Someone who is prone to discussion style will use a more linear approach. Likely to prefer that people speak one at a time, discussion-style leaders may go around the room in a team meeting, asking everyone to speak in turn. Engagement-style leaders, on the other hand, may be more comfortable with over-talking and being interrupted.

We have coached several African American leaders who have received feedback that their passion (translation: display of emotion) needs to be contained. In one situation, the young woman was the highest-ranking African American in the company. She was on the fast track. She developed a presentation about a very mundane compliance issue and decided to be creative in how she presented it. Rather than just sharing the facts, she developed a story about the topic using fictional characters.

After the presentation, she was under the impression that it had gone very well. However, a few days later, her manager shared that several of the senior leaders thought she should have just stayed with the facts. Her approach was inappropriate for the topic. At times, they said they thought they were listening to a Baptist preacher. This young woman's father, in fact, was a Baptist preacher and she acknowledged that unconsciously she may have mimicked some of his style. However, she was still hurt and frustrated because she felt even more alienated by her difference.

The Euro-American communication style relies heavily on logic and technical information rather than illusion, metaphor, and more creative and emotional styles of persuasion. Learning to communicate across cultures is a shared responsibility. In this case, if both had known more about culturally learned communication styles, they might have come to a different outcome.

Direct-communication cultures tend to be okay with voicing their unfiltered opinions. Indirect cultures may be very uncomfortable speaking up without having had some reflection time or speaking before a senior leader has spoken. Disagreeing with a superior might be considered disrespectful in some Asian cultures, whereas in discussion or engagement cultures, healthy debate is expected. Indirect cultures may not want criticism in public, whereas direct culture may be fine with public constructive feedback.

We have heard numerous times from Euro-American

leaders that their Asian employees tend not to speak up in meetings. Often their solution is to force everyone to speak via round-robin techniques. This approach may make some Asian employees and those from other indirect cultures very uncomfortable. When employees are reticent about speaking up in a meeting, discussion- or engagement-style leaders may see them as not conversant on the topic or disengaged.

Using the concepts of the DNA model outlined in Chapter 2, consider alternate interpretations for the behavior, for example, that these employees have a different cultural norm for engaging. The solution might be to expand the number of approaches for soliciting input (e.g., one-one or electronic forms of communication) and not making it mandatory that everyone speak during a group meeting.

In a study reported in *Harvard Business Review*, employees in a "speak-up" culture are 3.5 times as likely to contribute their full innovative potential.[42] However, we should consider alternative interpretations of what "speak up" means from a cultural perspective. It is critical, as part of your readiness for Bold, Inclusive Conversations, to have a basic understanding of culturally learned communication styles.

A cautionary note: We do not want to stereotype different groups. Not all African Americans communicate using engagement style; nor do all Asians prefer accommodation style. The explanation of the different styles is meant to help us understand that there are meaningful differences in how cultures communicate based on their norms, values, and beliefs. However, it does not mean that everyone who is a member of that group shares that characteristic. Some cultural groups, such as Native Americans, or Africans, may fall into any of the four styles, depending on factors including their history in terms of mobility and colonization.

BUILD CROSS-CULTURAL TRUST

There are myriad reasons for a lack of cross-cultural trust. Many historically marginalized groups have been taught not to trust the "other" based on historical atrocities, accounts of which have been passed down from generation to generation. "Never trust the white man" was a common admonition in my household growing up. I (Mary-Frances) was also taught not to trust or associate with anybody who practiced a religion different from my own because they were surely going to hell. And according to my mother, Jewish people could not be trusted to be honest. How many of us come to the workplace with embedded "records" that may now be deep in our unconscious minds but nonetheless drive our perceptions and behaviors?

We don't have to rely on history to understand the lack of trust between majority and minority groups. There are numerous modern-day examples of why trust is limited. African American communities may not trust police because of their firsthand experiences with racial profiling. Women may not trust leadership to provide equal benefits and pay.

By the same token, dominant group members may not trust historically marginalized groups because they don't know them very well or because of the single-story phenomenon mentioned earlier that perpetuates stereotypes, such as a low intelligence, lack of motivation (e.g., "Blacks are lazy"), and dishonesty (e.g., "You can't trust Arabs").

One of the key readiness steps before embarking on Bold, Inclusive Conversations is building trust. People will not talk honestly and openly when they have little or no trust. To build trust you need to consistently practice the 4-Es as outlined above. You cannot build trust without exposure to and experience with those who are different from you. How will you recognize trust between two people or among the team? One key sign is an openness to revealing and sharing personal information. Another sign of a trusting relationship is the willingness to be vulnerable—admitting weaknesses, acknowledging what you don't know.

In his *Harvard Business Review* article, "The Neuroscience of Trust," Paul Zak explores a study that compared people at low-trust companies with people at high-trust companies. Those at high-trust companies report 74 percent less stress, 106 percent more energy at work, 50 percent higher productivity, 13 percent fewer sick days, 76 percent more engagement, 29 percent more satisfaction with their lives, and 40 percent less burnout.[43] Through scientific brain studies and other research, he and his colleagues determined eight management behaviors that foster trust. Four are particularly pertinent to fostering Bold, Inclusive Conversations.

Share Information Broadly: If you do not have the whole picture (e.g., just a single story), it is impossible to have effective dialogue.

Intentionally Build Relationships: Exposure and experience with differences are critical components of Bold, Inclusive Conversations. The better I know you, the more I can trust you. We tend not to develop relationships across race, ethnicity, disability status, or sexual orientation in part due to the fear of the unknown and our human tendency to stay with our own tribe. Zak's research shows that when people intentionally build social ties at work, their performance improves. Finding common ground, as recommended in Chapter 2, can facilitate the ability to begin to build meaningful relationships across difference.

Show Vulnerability: The willingness on the part of leaders to admit when they do not know something builds credibility and trust, according to Zak's research. Some managers may find it more difficult to admit ignorance on topics like race and religion due to the fear of how it will look to their employees. They may feel as if they should know more than they do, and historically marginalized employees may feel the same. This is where patience and cutting each other some slack are important. When a manager genuinely shows interest and honestly admits to not knowing, it will likely engender more trust.

Facilitate Whole-Person Growth: We often define inclusion, in part, as the ability for individuals to bring their whole selves to work. Zak contends that assessing personal growth with discussions about work–life integration and family has a powerful effect on trust, as does allowing time for recreation and reflection, which improves engagement and retention. Leaders need to build skills to be comfortable talking about personal aspects with employees who are culturally different from them. I often hear from historically marginalized groups that such conversations feel awkward. We have a shared responsibility. Members of historically marginalized groups need to develop skills for the more personal conversations as well. Finding common ground, discussed in Chapter 2, is a good place to start.

According to Stephen Covey's book, *The Speed of Trust*, one of the core tenets of building trusting relationships is straight talk. "Say what is on your mind. Don't hide your agenda. When we talk straight, we tell the truth and leave the right impression."[44] While this may be sound advice, it doesn't work all of the time if you are from a historically marginalized group. Here are some reasons why straight talk is not always safe.

From the perspective of the historically marginalized group:

+ "If I tell you what it feels like to be a(n) _____ in this organization, you think I am whining or being overly sensitive."

+ "Straight talk will make you feel guilty or ashamed, and I don't want to make you feel bad. It could be a career derailer."

+ "I don't trust you with my straight talk. You would just not understand it, and I am not sure how you might share it or misinterpret it."

+ "If I say what is on my mind, I might lose my job."

+ "Nobody in this company really says what they think. I am not going to put myself out there."

+ "I am not the spokesperson for my identity group. You might use my perspective to generalize my group."

From the dominant-group perspective:

+ "To talk straight to you, I would have to admit that I really don't know anything about your group. I am embarrassed to admit that."

+ "I can't talk straight with you because you might get offended and file a lawsuit against the company."

+ "Nobody in this company really says what they think. I am not going to put myself out there."

Trust is built differently across cultures. Thomas Kochman in *Black and White Styles in Conflict* posited that African Americans tend to build trust via sharing their emotional reality in a direct manner and whites tend to build trust via controlling emotion. He found that Black people can trust if others are straight with them and share exactly what they think and feel. He found that white people built trust by sparing feelings to help keep the difficult conversation "on track."[45]

Such differences need to be acknowledged and understood to build mutual trust across differences. Experts agree that it takes years to build trust, seconds to break it, and forever to repair it. Building trust is a process—a journey—and not an event.

IS IT FACT OR TRUTH?

Facts can obscure the truth.

Maya Angelou[46]

Understanding the difference between fact and truth can help us to more effectively engage in Bold, Inclusive Conversations. While it might seem like splitting hairs, I think it is important to call out the distinction. Some will say, "Just the facts, please." Others will say, "What is my truth about this situation?" A fact is something that is undeniable and will stand until proven wrong. It is universally accepted. It is a fact that on January 6, 2021, thousands of people who claimed that the election of Joe Biden was ill-gotten angrily stormed the US Capitol, causing much damage and loss of life. Truth is much more subjective, incorporating feelings and beliefs, and it can change. Someone's truth about this event might be that it was necessary in an attempt to overturn an illegal election, while another's truth is that the election was legal, and the action amounted to an insurrection and the perpetrators should be punished accordingly.

Our perception of a situation is our truth. The example above may be so polarizing that conversation about it is not possible, and it may be best not to engage in order to preserve your well-being. Another example that might be somewhat easier to talk about is a woman who believes that she is not taken seriously for her contributions. This is her truth. This is what she experiences. She may have facts to substantiate her beliefs: incidences that have occurred—someone else got the promotion, for example. Her male boss thinks otherwise, based on his truth. The fact might be that over his career he has promoted a number of women. It does not change this woman's truth that she has not been promoted. It can be challenging to find common ground without sorting out the facts from someone's truth and recognizing that they are both important.

CAN WE SEPARATE THE PERSON FROM THE POSITION?

In the first edition we advocated for separating the person from the position. This is getting harder and harder to do; too often today the person's position causes harm to others. Sometimes there is a thin line between being inclusive of diverse views versus harmful positions. The goal should not be to accept all positions; rather, it is to be initially curious and open to understanding why someone might take a particular position before judging the person.

As an example, pro-choice versus pro-life perspectives have polarized this country. If you are pro-choice, can you respect a person who is pro-life? Can you disagree with someone's position without negatively labeling the person? If the person holding the pro-life viewpoint takes some action that harms others (e.g., attempting to stop individuals from entering abortion clinics, enacting laws that prevent women from seeking reproductive care), you would have grounds for judging the person's behavior. If, however, the person with the pro-life views exercises their belief as it relates to their own decisions and choices, and respects that others have the right to make different decisions and choices, perhaps we can then separate the person from the position.

A faction of powerful elected officials today are taking extreme positions against DEI such as transgender rights, reproductive rights, and race-based diversity. The motivation for these anti-inclusion views that harm many people appear to be personally motivated based on their own value system and not based on the will of the people who elected them. This makes it all but impossible to separate the person from the position and most likely impossible to engage in a Bold, Inclusive Conversation. Someone must believe in inclusion in order to have an inclusive conversation.

ASSESS ORGANIZATIONAL READINESS

The notion of culture certainly extends to organizational culture. So far, we have advised you to enhance your understanding of your own cultural norms and frameworks as well as those of others. Understanding the organizational culture is also key in assessing readiness to engage in Bold, Inclusive Conversations. How would you answer the following questions about your organization?

- Does it explicitly articulate inclusion as one of its values?
- Does it demonstrate that it values inclusion through actions by all leaders in the organization?
- Does it have formal programs in place promoting inclusion (e.g., employee network groups, mentoring, training, recruitment of diverse talent, etc.)?
- Does it celebrate diversity with different company-sponsored events?
- Does it actively support philanthropic causes of diverse groups?
- Do you see visible evidence of employee diversity?
- Are leaders evaluated on their inclusion practices?

◆ Does it have a culture of risk taking or risk aversion?

◆ Does it commonly call out the "elephants in the room" or does it tend not to tackle tough subjects?

◆ Would you characterize the culture as passive-aggressive?

◆ Do leaders show they care about all employees?

◆ Is the culture open or closed (i.e., few people allowed in the inner circle)?

◆ Are leaders well trained to support employee development and address relevant personal concerns?

◆ What is the level of trust of leadership?

If the culture does not demonstrate that it values all employees and incorporates inclusion as one of its core values, it may not be ready to tackle Bold, Inclusive Conversations.

As part of the readiness process, one organization assembled a small task force to evaluate the content of the dialogue session against the organizational culture. The initial content was designed to focus primarily on issues of race. The team determined that while race needed to be addressed as its own issue, the organization was not ready to tackle race by itself. This initial session would be more successful, they concluded, if they reframed it to encompass other diversity dimensions. The title was changed from Workplace Trauma in the Age of #BlackLivesMatter to Affirming Inclusion and Building Bridges during Challenging Times. Piloted with a group of HR and diversity leaders, the session was very successful, and the organization now plans to continue the dialogues, working up to discussing race, as well as a more comprehensive treatment of specific topics, such as LGBTQIA+ and religion.

You may think that you are personally ready to have Bold, Inclusive Conversations on polarizing topics, and you may also think that your organization needs to engage in these conversations because it would help to create a more inclusive climate. However, the facts may suggest otherwise. Tackling these topics before the organization is ready could be disastrous, leaving those involved feeling more alienated and polarized. In Chapter 2, we introduced the Intercultural Development Inventory and the Intercultural Developmental Continuum, which reveals that most people have a minimization mindset. A bold discussion on polarizing topics will likely be more successful with those who are at acceptance and adaptation on the continuum.

ARE YOU REALLY READY FOR BOLD, INCLUSIVE CONVERSATIONS?

After reading Chapters 2 and 3, you might be thinking, *If I have to do all of this to get ready to have a Bold, Inclusive Conversation, forget it. It is just too much work.*

Do not despair. If you have gotten through these chapters, you must have some level of interest in learning how to engage in bold conversations. Chapters 2 and 3 simply highlight the imperative of ensuring your readiness to engage in these difficult cross-cultural discussions and some of the important knowledge about others you need to have. Readiness is a journey. You do not have to wait until you have mastered all of the readiness skills before you start to have conversations across difference. At the very least, raise your self-awareness and your knowledge of the differences, as outlined in these two chapters, before attempting to engage in Bold, Inclusive Conversations. You will need to acknowledge your skill level (e.g., "I am new at this," "I don't know as much as I need to know about our differences," "I am still learning and hope you will support me in that journey"). As proven by Paul Zak's research highlighted earlier, showing

SURVEY 1. READINESS SELF-ASSESSMENT

		A great deal	Some-what	Not at all
1.	I am culturally self-aware.	☐	☐	☐
2.	I have explored my unconscious biases.	☐	☐	☐
3.	I am comfortable talking about difficult subjects.	☐	☐	☐
4.	I believe that treating everyone the same is not the solution to polarization.	☐	☐	☐
5.	I have studied my own and other cultures' norms and beliefs.	☐	☐	☐
6.	I have a high degree of emotional intelligence.	☐	☐	☐
7.	I readily acknowledge that I don't know what I don't know.	☐	☐	☐
8.	I recognize that there are differences that make a difference and I try not to minimize them.	☐	☐	☐
9.	I have regular exposure to difference.	☐	☐	☐
10.	I have meaningful relationships with diverse individuals and groups.	☐	☐	☐
11.	I can separate the person from their position.	☐	☐	☐
12.	My organizational culture is ready to have Bold, Inclusive Conversations.	☐	☐	☐
13.	There is a high level of trust in the organization.	☐	☐	☐
14.	There is a high level of trust within my team.	☐	☐	☐
15.	I am aware of my power and privilege.	☐	☐	☐
16.	I already have a lot of experience with Bold, Inclusive Conversations.	☐	☐	☐

your vulnerability and being willing to learn can go a long way in building trusting relationships.

Take the Readiness Self-Assessment survey (Survey 1) to gauge your readiness for Bold, Inclusive Conversations.

If you answered "somewhat" or "not at all" to all of the statements, you are definitely not ready to engage in polarizing conversations. If you answered "somewhat" or "not at all" to more than half of the statements, proceed with caution. If you were able to answer "a great deal" or "somewhat" to at least half of the statements, you can likely move more quickly through the steps provided in Chapters 5 and 6.

Simultaneously work on your readiness and move cautiously into the conversations, being mindful of how far your readiness will take you. As this is a skill, do not go beyond your capabilities, and continue to enhance them so that you can enjoy increasingly mutually beneficial interchanges across differences.

You might be wondering, *How long will it take to get ready?* We really don't know. As you can see from the self-assessment, it depends on a number of different factors. The key point is, if you are not ready, don't try to tackle the tough conversations. Go slowly and methodically. The remaining chapters provide guidance on the process.

CHAPTER 3 ◆ TIPS FOR TALKING ABOUT IT!

- ◆ **Learn about those who are different.** We may not have enough knowledge of cultural differences to effectively engage in Bold, Inclusive Conversations.

- ◆ **Learn to understand others from their worldview, not yours.** Learning about others from their perspective (i.e., having the ability to empathize) is key to forging mutual understanding.

◆ Remember that learning about others requires exposure, experience, education, and empathy.

◆ Engage in mutual or reciprocal learning. The need to expand our knowledge about the other is mutual.

◆ Recognize the importance of trust. Building trust across difference is a prerequisite to Bold, Inclusive Conversations.

◆ Learn how cultures differ in their communication styles to engage in Bold, Inclusive Conversations.

◆ As well as personal readiness, assess organizational readiness for Bold, Inclusive Conversations.

FOUR

Prepare: Why, Who, How, What, Where, and When?

Success depends upon previous preparation,
and without such preparation
there is sure to be failure.

CONFUCIUS

In Chapters 2 and 3, we explored readiness for Bold, Inclusive Conversations. This chapter will focus on preparation. Readiness is the ongoing learning process of becoming more knowledgeable about yourself and those who differ from you, whereas preparation is the plan for an impending conversation. We will explore the tactical aspects of preparing for the conversation in this chapter.

It is useful to use the Why, Who, How, What, Where, and When model often used in investigative reporting and other types of research as a template for getting prepared.

WHY ARE YOU HAVING BOLD, INCLUSIVE CONVERSATIONS?

The most critical question to consider is why are we pursuing a dialogue about "this"?

- What is the main reason for this particular bold, inclusive conversation?

- Why is this an important conversation to engage in? Why is it important to you? Do you think others you want to engage with will consider it as important?

- Is there pressure from certain individuals or groups to have this dialogue?

- Is it a part of what the organization normally does in the face of polarizing issues or would this be an exception to your organizational cultural norms?

- Is this a one-one performance feedback conversation?

- Is there a shared understanding of the purpose for the dialogue?

One organization decided to set up one-one conversations between senior leaders and BIPOC employees. The impetus for these conversations stemmed from a realization that employees of color were not being promoted at the same rate as their white counterparts. Leadership concluded that this was because they did not know the employees of color very well. They decided that holding 30-minute, individual get-to-know-you meetings would be a good first step.

The leaders responded positively to these meetings, indicating that they had gone very well. In contrast, the BIPOC employees were confused and, in some cases, anxious about the security of their jobs: "Why am I having this session with a senior leader? Am I in trouble?" The stated purpose of "just wanting to get to know you" left other employees wondering why and why now: "You have not wanted to get to know me before."

There was no shared understanding of the purpose of the meetings and it therefore resulted in skepticism and may have reduced trust in senior leaders on the part of BIPOC employees.

It is critical to clearly communicate the why and to ensure a shared meaning.

WHO WILL BE INVOLVED IN THE CONVERSATION AND WHY?

◆ Will this be a one-one conversation or will it involve a larger group?

◆ Is it an invitation or expectation that everyone will engage in the conversation?

◆ Who is convening the dialogue? Leadership? The communications department? HR? The Diversity and Inclusion Department? An employee affinity group?

◆ Will it be formal or more of an informal conversation?

◆ If a group, will it be an intact team discussion or will it be open to a larger group, many of whom may not know each other?

◆ Will all participants be on the same level in the organization or will managers and supervisors attend?

◆ What is the rationale for inviting or not inviting certain individuals or groups?

HOW WILL YOU ENGAGE IN BOLD, INCLUSIVE CONVERSATIONS?

It is important to consider what methods to use to convene Bold, Inclusive Conversations.

Pros and Cons of Virtual Gatherings

The first edition was written before the COVID-19 pandemic and offered pros and cons to virtual gatherings. While they are still valid, for a two-year period, most meetings convened virtually, which has now become an accepted norm. Prior to the COVID-19 pandemic only 8 percent of employees worked virtually. In 2022, 48 percent of employees worked virtually.[47] Zoom, Teams, and other platforms have become commonplace tools for all different types of gatherings, including training, town halls, team building, and regularly scheduled team meetings. Most employees now feel comfortable with virtual gatherings. They readily type their responses using the chat feature of the software. Even when we invite participants to come off mute to speak their opinions, many choose to type their comments.

One of the key advantages of large group (over 100) virtual dialogues is that participants can remain somewhat anonymous depending on who is participating and how they identify themselves (e.g., full name, first name only, pseudonym). This can also become a disadvantage because some might feel that it gives them license to make disparaging, inappropriate comments. This rarely happens during organization-sponsored sessions. However, during public virtual sessions, we sometimes need to close the written chat comments because of negative or harmful comments.

Another advantage of virtual sessions is that they can come together very quickly; participants can log in from almost anywhere. Virtual sessions can boost productivity, but on the flip side participants may use the opportunity to multitask and not stay focused on the sessions. We try to alleviate multitasking by incorporating polls and interspersing many discussion opportunities during sessions.

While virtual technology essentially allows us to do almost everything we would accomplish in face-to-face settings, including role-playing skill building exercises, we find it difficult to build relationships in virtual space. Technology malfunctions can also limit the effectiveness.

The same types of bias and microinequities present in

in-person meetings are also possible in virtual spaces, plus other biases unique to remote gatherings. We'll discuss microinequities in Chapter 8. A survey by Catalyst shows that, while leaders believe that working remotely has facilitated a more inclusive environment, employees tend to be less optimistic. When asked "Is your employer addressing the inequalities highlighted by the pandemic, such as racial and ethnic disparities?" 65 percent of business leaders said yes, versus 44 percent of employees. In addition, business leaders are also more likely to believe that their company is taking steps to enhance gender equity (56 percent) as compared with employees (34 percent).[48] The following types of biases are unique to virtual settings:

Camera Requirement: The requirement for camera use can disadvantage employees who may live in small spaces or may not have a background that they want to share. It could call out different socioeconomic statuses and/or show parts of an employee's private life that they would prefer to keep private. What is the decorum for "professional" on-camera appearance? Lactating mothers or employees caring for elders may be multitasking and find it difficult to always be camera ready. This does not mean they could not effectively engage with the camera off. If an organization deems it important to be on camera for some reason, it could provide a company background that everyone uses. Consider an option for being on camera for the start of the meeting or for group discussions, but give the option to be off camera during general information sharing or lectures.

Lack of Relationship Building: Employees in virtual settings do not interact much with others within their departments. In the absence of socialization, employees don't get opportunities for developing interpersonal bonds and friendships, which have been shown to reduce intergroup bias.[49] It is easier to have a Bold, Inclusive Conversation with someone with whom you already have a relationship.

Misinterpretation of the Written Word: The proclivity to write comments in chat can increase the potential of misunderstanding others. In an active chat, participants may miss key points because there are just too many comments coming in at once.

Technology Limitations: Virtual meeting technology and the technical difficulties that come with it, such as delayed audio, can make it harder for women and other minoritized groups to be heard. The larger the meeting size, the more the conversation tends to be dominated by a few individuals, making it even more difficult to contribute. It's also easier for colleagues to accidentally speak over each other in virtual meetings as compared to in-person meetings. According to a Catalyst survey, women were more likely to say they were talked over in virtual meetings.[50] In addition, historically marginalized groups may live in communities with slower internet service. According to an analysis by the nonprofit newsroom The Markup, the households with slower service are concentrated in lower-income communities with higher populations of BIPOC.[51]

Hybrid Meetings

According to research by Gartner, in 2023 it was estimated that 39 percent of the global workforce was hybrid. In the United States, 74 percent of companies have implemented or plan to implement a hybrid model. Post pandemic, many organizations mandated that employees come back into the office for some part of the work week. In the United States, 86 percent of Latine knowledge workers and 81 percent of

Asian/Asian American and Black knowledge workers would prefer a hybrid or fully remote work arrangement, compared with 75 percent of white knowledge workers. Globally, 52 percent of women want to work at least mostly remotely versus 46 percent of men. And 50 percent of working moms report they'd prefer to work from home most or all of the time, as compared to 43 percent of working dads.[52]

There are reasons that historically excluded and marginalized groups prefer a remote or hybrid work arrangement in addition to the obvious benefits for everyone. There are fewer direct microinequities and microaggressions, allowing BIPOC to focus on the work and not the politics and social discomfort associated with **code-switching.**

The risk of this new working arrangement is that we create "us-and-them" cultures where in-person workers are advantaged over those working virtually. If decision-makers spend more time in the office, they may favor those who are in close physical proximity. Here are some tips for hybrid meetings.

- Be mindful of holding spontaneous in-office meetings that might exclude those working virtually.

- Be intentional in setting meeting times that consider the schedules of both in-office and virtual workers.

- Include non-work-related check-ins (this may only work for smaller teams) at the beginning of meetings to show care and concern for the well-being of the team, keeping in mind that employees have different personal circumstances.

- Reduce the number of meetings. "Zoom fatigue" is real. Consider whether you need a full-blown meeting or if you can use other technology collaboration tools, such as an instant messaging platform like Slack.

- Ensure that remote employees have as much voice as in-person workers.
- For large groups (more than twenty-five), a hybrid setting is likely not the best to discuss polarizing topics.

We must also keep in mind that many workers do not have the option of working virtually. They have jobs that require their physical presence. These include providing care, operating machinery, using lab equipment, and processing customer transactions in stores.

Disproportionately, these types of jobs are held by BIPOC.[53] And often their voices are not included in Bold, Inclusive Conversations. We work with clients to find creative ways to include workers who cannot leave their machines or workplaces (e.g., hospital workers) to come to a dialogue on polarizing topics. One client paid for overtime to include everyone in the conversation at the end of their shift. However, this did not solve the issue completely, as some workers had personal obligations that precluded them from staying beyond their regularly scheduled hours.

In-Person Sessions

The traditional way of convening people may still be the most effective for Bold, Inclusive Conversations. From a perception perspective, some people may feel that in-person sessions are more personal and send a signal that you as a leader care more about the topic/issue and their feelings about it.

Another advantage to meeting in person is the ability to assess tone and body language, which virtual settings make difficult. In-person sessions also more readily lend themselves to team and relationship building with groups who may not already know each other.

Initial sessions with the purpose of listening or raising awareness can be successfully accomplished using virtual methods. However, for more difficult topics, face-to-face may still be preferable.

The Town Hall Example

In an attempt to quell fears and reaffirm its commitment to DEI, an organization decided to have a town hall meeting to discuss some recent tragic events, including terrorist attacks, workplace shootings, and the killings of unarmed Black men. The session was open to everyone. Inasmuch as this organization routinely held town hall meetings facilitated by the CEO or other senior leaders, there was good attendance from a cross-section of employees from different backgrounds and different areas of the company.

However, unlike other town hall meetings where employees readily engaged in the conversation, there was uncomfortable silence during this meeting. Afterward the organizers realized that employees did not share their thoughts on these topics because of the level of polarization. They were fearful that their opinions would be judged and criticized in front of leaders and coworkers.

Town hall–style meetings can be effective. Be clear on the purpose. Is it to share information and reaffirm commitment with little expectation that employees will engage? If the goal is engagement, maybe set it up with smaller group breakouts. Or you might consider convening intentional intact team discussions following the town hall session.

Affinity Group Example

Another organization decided to take a different approach. The Winters Group was invited to facilitate a two-hour session with the African American employee affinity group to discuss the stress that the killings of unarmed Black men was causing among its members. The purpose of the meeting was twofold: (1) to share feelings and (2) to develop skills to effectively discuss these topics. Initially, we planned to invite senior leaders, who could hear the frustration and concern among the African American employees. However, we decided that the first session might be more effective if it included only the affinity group members. This approach allowed for a more open dialogue than might have been achieved if the session had been open to leaders. The employees of this organization are quite dispersed, and while a number had independently shared their frustrations with the affinity group leader, there had not been an opportunity for members to hear from each other.

During this first session, it became apparent that we needed another session with just the African American employee affinity group because we were only able to accomplish the first objective of sharing feelings. Emotions were still too raw to try to work on the skill-building portion of the agenda.

During the second session, a recommendation surfaced to hold a third gathering that would include other employee network groups (e.g., Latine, Asian, LGBTQIA+) as well as members of the diversity council. This particular council was comprised of some senior leaders in the organization. The purpose of the combined session was to be more inclusive and explore other issues that might be causing stress for these groups (e.g., fear of being deported, Islamophobia concerns). The third, combined session surfaced new issues, such as the young gay Muslim man's fear of standing too close to the edge of the track at the metro station, discussed in Chapter 1.

During this meaningful dialogue we were able to talk about specific skills such as meeting people where they are (e.g., using the Intercultural Development Continuum model to assess the level of competency as outlined in Chapter 3), managing emotions, using "I" statements, and listening. Chapter 5 will embellish on these skills.

Affinity Group Example 2

A different organization had difficulty initially getting approval to hold a dialogue session with their African American affinity group employees. The leadership did not want to endorse a discussion about topics that had historically been discouraged in the workplace. Conceding that the proliferation of tragic events constituted extraordinary circumstances, the session was approved, but only if the most senior African American leaders would be present and if it was open to all employees.

Again, The Winters Group was invited to facilitate the session. The presence of African American senior leadership was very impactful. The highest-ranking African American leader spoke on behalf of all senior leaders, and employees felt encouraged that senior leaders attended to listen. The group decided that this was the first in what should be ongoing dialogues about timely topics that might disrupt their ability to be totally present doing their best work.

There are pros and cons to including different levels within the organization in the sessions. On the one hand, the presence of leaders offers a greater likelihood that some type of action will result, if that is one of the goals. Additionally, leaders hear employees' perceptions firsthand. The disadvantage is that employees may be less candid in the presence of senior leadership. The key is knowing who to invite at what point in the conversation. That will depend on a number of factors, including the purpose of the meeting (e.g., raising awareness, listening, brainstorming, skill building), readiness, and organizational norms (e.g., is it customary to hold multi-level meetings?).

Leverage Employee Affinity Groups

The impetus for the conversations referenced above came from employee affinity groups. Utilizing such existing networks can be very effective in organizing Bold, Inclusive Conversations. Employee affinity group members are in tune with the issues facing their respective groups, have already been sanctioned by the company, and therefore have some level of credibility and leverage. A senior leader in the organization, who often comes from a different identity group (e.g., African American network sponsors were white men for the sessions), generally sponsors one or more of the organization's affinity groups.

Typically, the sponsor's role is to advise and support the group in achieving its goals. For the sessions described here, the sponsor opened the meeting with an overview of the importance of the conversation and shared a message that leadership wanted to ensure that all employees felt valued and included. The sponsor said that his primary role during the conversation was to listen and answer any direct questions that participants might have.

If your organization does not have employee affinity groups, you may have a diversity council or committee that can be very helpful in organizing Bold, Inclusive Conversations. If you don't have a group already in place, perhaps approach well-respected senior leaders who might support such conversations.

Caucus Groups

A specific type of affinity group called a caucus is used in racial justice work. These convenings offer opportunities for those who share the same identity group to meet separately to gather, connect, and learn.[54] Caucuses based on racial identity provide an opportunity for BIPOC, white people, and multi-racial people to meet separately to intentionally discuss their racial identities. These are spaces for learning and building more self-awareness of the role of race in our lives. Some of our clients have resisted using the caucus methodology because they believe it fuels divisiveness. This can be a valid concern. However, if the caucus sessions are devised well by clearly articulating the why, they can be very beneficial. The rationale for caucus groups includes the following:

◆ Organizations may not be ready for mixed-group dia-logue. As mentioned in the affinity group example above, it was critical for the African American employees to have time to meet and process before inviting others into the dialogue.

◆ They can alleviate the fear of speaking up in mixed groups, and therefore more shared learning and under-standing may take place.

◆ They can be likened to understanding a system. You sometimes need to disaggregate the whole to understand its parts and then bring the pieces together. White people need to enhance their awareness of the role that their racial identity plays in organizational systems. BIPOC identity groups each have had different histories in US dominant cultural settings. Having a clearer, collective understanding of those dynamics can support Bold, Inclusive Conversations.

Who Should Facilitate?

Another important who question is Who will facilitate the session? Will it be an internal HR person or an external consultant? One client, the chief diversity officer of a large financial institution, decided to facilitate an open dialogue herself. She shared that it went very well. It was open to all employees and more than 100 participated. The purpose of the dialogue was to raise awareness of the potential impact of the external tragedies on employees.

The advantage of an internal facilitator is that the person is likely well known in the organization, which might lead to a more candid dialogue. On the other hand, outside facilitators can bring facilitation skills as well as experience from other client settings and perhaps a more neutral, less threatening presence.

It is critical for group sessions to engage an experienced facilitator to guide the session. Of course in a one-one session, there would be no need for a third party, unless the circumstances warranted it (e.g., the person asking for the Bold, Inclusive Conversation wants an advocate or ally in the room, or there is need for translation or other accommodations).

WHAT IS THE EXPECTED OUTCOME?

The next question after why and who is What do we want to achieve during this dialogue? Many of us are trained to move as swiftly as possible from problem identification to problem solving. However, topics such as race, religion, and politics are complex and do not lend themselves easily to popular problem-solving models such as assess, plan, do (take action), evaluate. This type of model is a good starting point for a dialogue framework. Expect that the assessment and planning parts may take longer and require more readiness than for noncontroversial topics, such as how you will fix a software glitch. The company mentioned earlier in this chapter that decided to hold 30-minute one-one meetings as a means of getting to know employees of color offers an example of not spending enough time on assessing and planning before getting to action.

Effective assessment requires readiness and, as pointed out in Chapters 1 and 2, readiness takes time. Before you even think about doing, take the time to adequately assess and plan. Many businesspeople have been taught to be action oriented: What are we going to do about this? We want to get to solutions as quickly as possible so we can get on with it or get to the next problem. This sense of urgency is often associated with dominant group culture characteristics and in excess it can exacerbate rather than solve the issue. Consider the short-term desired outcome as well as what you want to achieve in the longer term.

The short-term outcome of a Bold, Inclusive Conversation might simply be to listen and share perspectives. Ground rules for the first conversation might include no debating, no criticizing, and asking questions for clarification only. In our first affinity group example, we learned very soon into the first session that our agenda was too full. There was no way in two hours that we would be able to listen and also do some skill building. We realized that this group just wanted and, quite frankly, just needed to talk—to share with each other how the events such as the killings of unarmed Black men, people being targeted because of their religion—were impacting them and their ability to focus on their job responsibilities. We should have had no other expected outcome for that initial session other than sharing.

The why, who, how, what for more dialogue sessions may organically unfold. In the example referenced above, the group decided during the second meeting that they should expand their efforts to include additional employee affinity groups.

What? So What? Now What? Analysis

A useful tool for planning and developing an agenda of expected outcomes for each session is a framework that asks What? So what? Now what? For example, based on the situation described above:

◆ **What?** A session to share feelings about recent tragic events.

◆ **So what?** Acknowledgment of similar emotional responses can be cathartic and validating and as a result we gain some level of healing and improve our well-being.

◆ **Now what?** Expand our dialogue to include other affinity groups.

The agenda for each conversation should be written and provided to each participant. The agenda should clearly stipulate what will and will not be discussed during that particular conversation. However, I have found that cultures from the oral tradition of communication (e.g., African American, Latine, Native American) might not feel bound by the written agenda and will be more apt to let the conversation go where it goes. It is important to have a good facilitator who can steer the group back to the agenda or at least confirm that they want to change the agenda.

WHERE SHOULD BOLD, INCLUSIVE CONVERSATIONS TAKE PLACE?

While this is not a concern for virtual sessions except when participants come together in the same physical space, for in-person sessions, place matters.

◆ Is the room the right size?

◆ How is the room configured?

- What environmental concerns (heating, air conditioning, noise level) might there be?
- Is the space easily accessible to people with physical differences such as hearing or visual impairments?
- Will the setting be comfortable for people with different body sizes?

Several of the places selected for in-person sessions have been less than ideal. In one case the room was way too small, and in another, the room was way too big. One of our sessions took place in a large auditorium that probably seated 500 people; we had about 25 in attendance. It did not create a conducive atmosphere for open, inclusive dialogue. One time the room was freezing and there seemed to be no remedy. Another session met in a room that was way too hot. One memorable session took place in a room that was very hard to find, and many participants arrived late and a bit frustrated.

While we recognize that many of the place considerations may be out of the control of those organizing the dialogue, we mention these items because, with an already emotionally charged topic, you will want to manage as many of the logistical aspects as you can. The success of the meeting will be influenced by these factors. We have heard comments like: "They put us in the worst room possible. Another sign that they just don't care. We are not that important." Or "The room is so far away. I wonder if they did that on purpose, to discourage us from attending." When little trust or maybe even some paranoia exists, you will want to be proactive in considering how to alleviate such perceptions.

An ideal configuration for the room setup might be a circle of chairs with no table, or a U-shape that allows participants to see each other. Theater-style arrangements might seem too

TEMPLATE 1. PLANNING TOOL
FOR BOLD, INCLUSIVE CONVERSATIONS

	Conversation 1	*Conversation 2*
Why are we having this conversation?		
Who should be invited?		
What is the desired outcome (e.g., listening, creating shared meaning, probing differences)?		
How should the conversation be conducted? (In-person, virtual)		
Where and when should we hold the conversation?		
How will the room be set up (if in person); with what technology?		
How many sessions are anticipated?		
Who will facilitate the session?		

TEMPLATE 1 (continued)

	Conversation 3	*Conversation 4*
Why are we having this conversation?		
Who should be invited?		
What is the desired outcome (e.g., listening, creating shared meaning, probing differences)?		
How should the conversation be conducted? (In-person, virtual)		
Where and when should we hold the conversation?		
How will the room be set up (if in person); with what technology?		
How many sessions are anticipated?		
Who will facilitate the session?		

formal and require those who wish to speak to stand up and face as many of the participants as possible; however, their back would still be to some participants unless they moved to the front of the room, which might make some speakers uncomfortable. The configuration depends on the type of forum (e.g., town hall style versus smaller, more intimate gathering) and the purpose of the meeting. There is no one right answer. However, we recommend that you proactively consider room setup.

See the planning template for assistance in preparing for a Bold, Inclusive Conversation (Template 1).

WHEN SHOULD YOU HAVE BOLD, INCLUSIVE CONVERSATIONS?

Obviously it is important to minimize what may be perceived as an impact on productivity. All of the in-person sessions that we have facilitated occurred after normal work hours. In one case the session was held from 5:30–7:30 p.m. with a light dinner provided. Another client chose 4:00–6:00 p.m. Some of the virtual sessions were conducted during lunch times such as 11:30–1:00 p.m. and marketed as "lunch and learns," while others were convened during early morning time slots such as 8:00–9:30 a.m.

Another issue relates to "on-time starts." A number of sessions, both in-person and virtual, have not started on time due to late arrivals. You will want to consider how much after the start time is acceptable. It can be disruptive if participants arrive too late. I would suggest stating in the invitation that no one will be admitted after (state time).

Another important consideration is time zones. For organizations with employees dispersed throughout the country and/or the world, you should consider the most convenient time for most and/or hold the same session more than once at different times. Also consider the time zone for the facilitator.

PREPARING FOR ONE-ONE CONVERSATIONS

This chapter has focused on planning for group conversations. If the Bold, Inclusive Conversation will take place between just you and one other person, most of the advice still holds, with a few caveats on how and when and where. I would recommend that one-one conversations of this nature not be conducted virtually, if possible, at least for the first conversation. It is important to establish a connection that would be difficult to do in a virtual setting. If meeting in person is not possible, acknowledge the limitations of the technology up front and try to find a way to meet in person soon after this initial session. Relative to when, it may not be wise to hold a one-one session after normal working hours as such timing may send a message that this is a lesser priority.

Consider this true example: A certain employee becomes very anxious before her performance evaluations. Her palms get sweaty and she barely hears what her manager says because she is so nervous. The next year, rather than conduct the performance review in an office setting with the desk between them, the manager invited the employee for coffee. As they walked to the company cafeteria, they chatted. When they sat down, the manager changed the subject and started to talk about a nonwork topic. When the employee asked about her performance review, the manager responded, "We had it on the way to the cafeteria."

Changing the venue significantly reduced this employee's anxiety level. While a performance discussion is not necessarily a polarizing topic, *where* matters even more for those discussions. A formal office setting with a desk between the two parties can establish a power dynamic that hinders open dialogue. More informal, casual, neutral settings might break down physical and emotional barriers, enhance openness, and support a feeling of equity.

AVOID SPONTANEOUS, UNPLANNED CONVERSATIONS

The advice in this chapter has focused on how to prepare for Bold, Inclusive Conversations. Sometimes you may find yourself in a situation where a difficult topic that you have not prepared for comes up spontaneously. Perhaps a polarizing topic such as race, religion, or politics just comes up in a meeting, or you overhear a negative comment about your identity group while in the break room, or somebody asks you a question about your stance on a political issue that takes you by surprise. What should you do then? If there is no way to prepare, your response depends on a number of factors including:

◆ Your relationship with the individual(s): How well do you know them?

◆ Are you the manager or a coworker?

◆ Have you had Bold, Inclusive Conversations with them before?

◆ Is there time to adequately address the topic?

◆ What is your emotional state?

◆ What is their emotional state?

Nine times out of ten, you will want to discourage spontaneous conversation on these difficult topics. You might say: "That is an interesting question/perspective/comment and to fully address it, I need some time to think about it. Can we table this and talk about it when we have more time to fully address it?" If the response is, "No, I would like to talk about it now," continue to push back: "I understand that this is an important discussion. I want to be prepared. I hope that you can understand that. Let's schedule a time to delve into this in more detail."

CHAPTER 4 ◆ TIPS FOR TALKING ABOUT IT!

◆ Preparation is different from readiness. Readiness is the longer-term process of introspection and learning more about those who are different from you, as outlined in Chapters 2 and 3. Preparation is getting ready for impending Bold, Inclusive Conversations.

◆ In preparation consider the why, who, how, what, where, and when of the conversations. Use the planning tool (Template 1) as a guide.

◆ Virtual sessions can be as effective as in-person sessions depending on the why, what, and who.

◆ In-person sessions may be more effective for one-one Bold, Inclusive Conversations than virtual formats.

◆ In general, try to avoid spontaneous, unplanned conversations on polarizing topics.

Focus on Self- and Other-Understanding
- Explore the role of identity, cultural competence, bias, and fear

Assess Readiness
- Engage in 4-Es
- Gauge individual and organizational readiness

Prepare for the Conversation
- Identify the Why, Who, How, What, Where, and When

Create Shared Meaning
- Establish common group based on facts and data

Delve Deep Into Differences
- Acknowledge polarization
- Engage in reciprocal learning

Interpret and Bridge
- Sharpen inclusive habits

Reflect and Learn

Reflect and Learn

THE BOLD, INCLUSIVE CONVERSATIONS MODEL

◆ ◆ ◆

FIVE

Let the Conversations Begin: Search for Shared Meaning

When we listen with curiosity, we don't listen with the intent to reply. We listen for what's behind the words.

ROY T. BENNETT

Now that you have a better understanding of the prerequisites for having Bold, Inclusive Conversations and you have assessed your readiness, let's turn our attention to the actual conversation.

Remember, this is a process and not a singular event. (See Figure 1 from the Introduction, repeated here for your convenience.) You may need to hold several conversations that build on one another to reach the desired outcome of shared meaning and ultimately the ability to deeply understand each other's perspectives, which we explore in Chapter 6. If you and the other(s) engaging in the conversation already have experience, perhaps one conversation will suffice, depending on the topic and the desired outcomes. This chapter primarily addresses those with limited skills to have Bold, Inclusive Conversations, and therefore assumes that multiple conversations will be necessary. Use your judgment as to how many conversations you may need in your situation.

GUIDANCE FOR THE FIRST CONVERSATION

Let's look at the following scenario and work through the process at a high level for what might happen at the first meeting. Jake is a white manager. Rodney, an African American, reports to Jake. Rodney has come to ask Jake why the company has not taken a visible position on the recent killings of African American men. Rodney shares that these situations have left him anxious and fearful, and he has overheard other white employees being dismissive about these incidents. Rodney asks for Jake's advice. He suggests that maybe the team should get together to talk about it.

Note: While this example is about race because it is one of the most difficult topics, you can substitute other polarizing subjects and use this same process.

As the Manager, What Should You Do?

Jake suggests a one-one meeting with Rodney at another mutually convenient time before he agrees to convene a group session. Do not attempt the conversation without the readiness and preparation outlined in the previous chapters.

At this juncture, many managers will feel anxious and may want to bring in someone from Human Resources or the legal department to be a part of the initial discussion. Please resist that temptation as the first thing you would do. Often when the topic is about some group that is protected by law (e.g., race, gender, age, sexual orientation, disability), our immediate concern is the legal vulnerability. Many managers have been taught to mitigate risks by consulting with HR or legal, which are invaluable resources to the organization. However, sometimes managers would rather hand over these types of issues to one of these departments. As the first step, managers should gather more information before engaging any other stakeholders.

Rodney may feel even more vulnerable and marginalized if others become involved before he has an opportunity to share his perspectives. He may not see this as a legal issue at all. Rodney may simply want to have a candid conversation with Jake to talk about a topic that concerns him. Bringing in legal counsel or someone from HR could diminish the possibility of establishing a trusting relationship, as Rodney may feel that Jake thinks he may be contemplating a legal action against the company, which in turn can shut down the possibility of conversation altogether. He may think that Jake considers him a legal risk just because he's Black. You can well imagine how these assumptions can negatively impact trust.

A real organization faced a similar situation. An African American HR manager met with the white senior vice-president of HR to share that African American employees in her division of the company did not feel that they were being treated with the same respect as their white counterparts. They did not feel included. The African American HR manager simply wanted to discuss the concerns with her boss. However, on the advice of their internal legal department, the company immediately decided to hire an external law firm to conduct a full investigation of the situation without further discussion or consultation with the HR manager who brought the concerns to leadership. This left the African American HR manager feeling frustrated, ignored, and excluded.

While the HR manager did not think that it was necessary to involve legal counsel, company policy might have dictated that action on matters relating to race, gender, and other groups protected by law. In the situation above in which Rodney wants to discuss the situation with Jake, Rodney could ask Jake not to involve others at this juncture.

Rodney might say, "I realize that given the nature of my concern and that we don't typically discuss these topics at work, it may be company policy to engage HR and/or legal. Is it possible for just the two of us to have a conversation first? And then you can let me know if you feel you need to go outside the department."

As the manager, Jake should learn as much as he can about the different perspectives on the topic before his scheduled conversation with Rodney. Jake might want to consult HR for guidance but not have a representative present at this initial meeting. Before meeting with Rodney, Jake should prepare by doing the following:

- Explore his own perspectives and question why he feels as he does about the issue.

- Learn about the topic from other perspectives.

- Assess how much trust there is with Rodney by considering previous situations that might have either built or eroded trust.

- Establish that the purpose of the meeting is for him to listen to Rodney.

- Consider his own conflict resolution style as discussed in Chapter 3. Is it engagement, discussion, accommodation, or dynamic? Consider Rodney's conflict resolution style.

Rodney should also prepare. Before meeting with Jake, he should do the following:

- Learn as much as he can about different perspectives on the situation for his own understanding.

- Explore his own perspectives and question why he feels as he does.

- Learn as much as he can about the topic from the perspectives of others.

- Assess how much trust there is with Jake by considering previous situations that might have built or eroded trust.

- Ask himself if he believes that Jake, as a white man, really would not understand how he feels, and if so, what evidence there is of this. Consider how he will effectively engage in the conversation if he feels this way. Plan to share information that might enhance Jake's understanding.

- Consider his conflict resolution style as discussed in Chapter 3. Is it engagement, discussion, accommodation, or dynamic? Consider Jake's conflict resolution style.

CONVERSATION 1:
JAKE LISTENS TO RODNEY

The recommendations outlined for this conversation assume that both Rodney and Jake are new at having Bold, Inclusive Conversations. See Chapter 6 for Am I Ready?, a guide for assessing where to start the conversation.

Considering Rodney initiated the conversation, Jake's role should be just to listen, not to interject his opinion or to debate. The specific goals of the first meeting might include the following:

Create a "Brave Zone": A brave zone encompasses a safe zone but goes further because it gives you permission to be courageous in saying things that might be uncomfortable.

Agree on Confidentiality Parameters: Jake might say something like: "This conversation is just between us at this point. If I feel that I have to escalate your concerns, I will let you know first, and we can talk about the best way to move forward."

Enhance Jake's Understanding: These topics are very personal and are often at the core of our identity. As highlighted in Chapter 3, we don't understand if we have not had the employee's experience. Therefore Jake should refrain from saying, "I understand how you feel." Rather, he should say something like, "I want to better understand how you may be feeling and how this is impacting you at work."

Rodney Shares His Perspective: Rodney should not expect Jake to have solutions at this juncture or even understand all of his perspective. Rodney should assume positive intent and make sure he balances his presentation between his perspective and the facts as he knows them. He should not point out blame or be judgmental. He should try to present in as neutral a way as possible and avoid saying things like, "I don't think most white people understand." Instead, he should say something like, "I know that it's sometimes hard for me to understand issues that may not impact me directly and this may be hard for you too." (Here Rodney uses an "I" statement, in an attempt to not put Jake on the defensive.)

Recognize Cultural Differences in Communication Styles: Rodney's culture may be more or less emotionally expressive than Jake's. For certain cultures, too much emotional display is off-putting. For other cultures, too little emotional display suggests you don't care, as discussed in Chapter 3. Rodney should find the balance that will work while still being authentic. It will be important for Rodney to use "I" language and not speak for others who share his identity. For example, he should not say: "I think I speak for all African Americans on the team." Rodney can only speak for himself unless he has actually spoken to others and has their permission to share their perspectives.

Foster Dialogue, Not Debate: People commonly use debate to persuade others toward one idea over another. We learn how to debate in school and politics. Debating has its use but not when it comes to engaging in Bold, Inclusive Conversations. By their very nature, debates are oppositional—two sides, each attempting to prove the other wrong by searching for the weaknesses in the other's perspective and implying that there is only one right answer: theirs. The objective of a dialogue is the exact opposite: collaborative working toward common ground, searching for the strengths in another's perspective, and assuming more than one right answer. A dialogue strives for a win-win solution.

Rodney might present some of the following facts:

- The imprisonment rate of Black males is 5.3 times higher than that of white males.[55]

- Although 27 percent of the people fatally shot by police are Black[56], Black people account for only 13.6 percent of the population.[57]

- According to the US Bureau of Justice Statistics, Black people account for 35 percent of the total prison population, a disproportionate representation given Census numbers.[58]

Next, Rodney may share his personal experience:

- I realize that the reasons for these statistics are complex including unconscious bias, poverty, education, historical exclusion (e.g., job discrimination, redlining), and violence in many urban Black communities.

- I have personally been stopped by police despite not breaking the law. In the Black community this is known as "driving while Black."

- Every time I hear of another shooting, I become more fearful, not only for myself but also for my son.

The facts are critical, but as stated earlier, understanding individual experiences—one's truth—is also key.

Listen: Jake's role during this conversation is to simply listen. I think there is universal agreement that the key to effective dialogue is listening. Listening to understand when the topics are polarizing requires more intentionality. Most experts posit that most of us listen to defend or reply rather than to understand. It is really important to listen only for understanding, especially during the first session.

How Do You Listen to Understand?

- When you find yourself disagreeing or wanting to debate a point, stop and ask yourself why. Commit to yourself that you will explore your contrary opinion later during the reflection phase (outlined later in this chapter) and quickly get back to listening.

- Make a mental note, rather than written notes, of those things that you don't understand. However, if you really feel that you must write things down as a reminder to yourself, make sure you ask for permission to take notes and to let the employee know that they are for your own research and follow-up.

- Individuals from historically marginalized groups may have a hard time believing that someone from the dominant group has positive intent. Huge trust issues may exist that make meaningful conversation more difficult. Jake can demonstrate positive intent with body language that demonstrates that he is engaged and listening.

- Ask clarifying questions. "Could you tell me more about that? I did not understand your last point. Could you elaborate?"

These techniques will provide evidence that you are really listening to understand.

Expect Nonclosure at the First Conversation: You actually want nonclosure at this juncture. It is simply a conversation where Jake will practice intense listening and Rodney will practice sharing from his perspective. The conversation might end with Jake saying something like, "Thank you for sharing your perspective, Rodney. I really learned a lot and now would like some time to reflect on what you said and perhaps do some more learning. Can we agree to meet again in two weeks?" Jake should leave enough time to do his homework but not so much that Rodney feels ignored.

Rodney should be prepared to recommend resources to support Jake in gaining greater knowledge about the issues facing African Americans in the criminal justice system, such as the books *A People's History of the United States,*[59] *The History of White People,*[60] *Justice in America: The Separate Realities of Blacks and Whites,*[61] *The New Jim Crow: Mass Incarceration in the Age of Colorblindness,*[62] *Stamped from the Beginning,*[63] *Black Fatigue,*[64] *The Sum of Us*[65] and the Netflix documentary *13th.*[66] This will support Jake in better understanding the contextual implications for the facts that Rodney has shared.

Following the First Conversation:
Reflect and Learn

It will be important for both Jake and Rodney to reflect on the outcome of the first conversation before moving forward.

Jake should ask himself:

◆ How did I feel about the conversation?

◆ What did I learn?

◆ What did I disagree with and why?

◆ What surprised me and why?

◆ What else do I need to learn about before I have the next conversation?

Rodney should ask himself:

◆ How did I feel about the conversation?

◆ Was Jake really listening? What were the clues that he was/was not listening?

◆ Was my presentation clear, concise, and cohesive?

◆ How did my natural engagement communication style show up? Was I able to balance my emotional expressiveness, knowing that Jake uses a discussion style?

◆ Did I just talk about my opinion, or was I balanced with my perspective and facts as I know them?

◆ Are there points of clarification that I need to get more information about? What else do I need to learn before the next conversation?

They might both also want to seek advice from a colleague or friend who may be more skilled at understanding these issues while maintaining any confidentiality agreements they created.

CONVERSATION 2:
SEARCHING FOR SHARED MEANING

The second conversation has two objectives: (1) for Jake to share what he has learned and ask more questions as necessary, and (2) to search for shared understanding. Rodney's role during the first part of the second conversation is primarily to listen to Jake, using all of the listening guidelines outlined above, and answer the questions posed in the last conversation and during the reflection and learning period. During the second part of this conversation, their goal is to try to find common ground—to get to a place of shared meaning.

Conversation 2, Phase 1:
Jake Shares, Rodney Listens

Jake should ask questions to clarify Rodney's perspective as a result of his additional knowledge garnered during the reflection and learning period. Jake might say, "I really appreciated our last meeting. I have had time to reflect and learn more. I have some additional questions, if you don't mind. I admit that I am new to understanding the complexities of race. I do want to learn more, so I hope you'll bear with me if you think some of my questions are naïve or uninformed or just plain stupid."

Rodney might say, "I think I sometimes expect others to know more about the issues of my culture than they do, and I also sometimes resent having to be the teacher. This is something I'm working on, so if I seem impatient or assume that you should already know something, I ask that you are patient with me."

Jake could respond, "Great—we can be patient with each other."

This type of exchange helps to build common ground as well as trust. Each party admits the need to learn something (i.e., they have something in common). Their willingness to be vulnerable in this regard helps to build trust.

Exercise Patience and Understanding

We often hear from employees from historically marginalized groups that they are tired of educating whites about the issues that they face. The sentiment goes something like this: "After all of these years of racial strife in this county, white people should get it. I am tired of trying to teach white people what it is like."

This is a real consideration, and it should be a choice for BIPOC to teach dominant-group people about our experiences. It can burden and retraumatize BIPOC, and it is okay for Rodney to want to set boundaries. In this situation, Rodney has agreed to be a teacher.

It is important to note that Rodney's capacity to be patient and understanding of Jake's inexperience will depend on Rodney's emotional state. It is critical that Rodney assess his ability to engage patiently and productively. At this point, he should take our self-assessment, Are You Ready to Get to Shared Meaning?

Conversation 2, Phase 2:
Getting to Shared Meaning

The conversation should now transition to getting to shared understanding. The **Ladder of Inference**, as shown in Figure 8, is a helpful model for understanding the complexities associated with trying to find common ground.

We need to recognize that while the same pool of data may be available to everyone, we may select data on the basis of our identity group, biases, our worldview, and what we hold as important. We therefore draw interpretations based on our assumptions about what is true or not.

These assumptions and interpretations lead us to actions based on our beliefs. The DNA model highlighted in Chapter 2 can also be useful at this stage of the dialogue.

Let's apply the DNA model to one of the issues Rodney raised. One of the behaviors Rodney describes is the rising number of unarmed Black men who have been killed by police. Possible interpretations include (1) Black men are more likely to be criminals, (2) racism leads to this outcome, and (3) racial disproportionality in the criminal justice

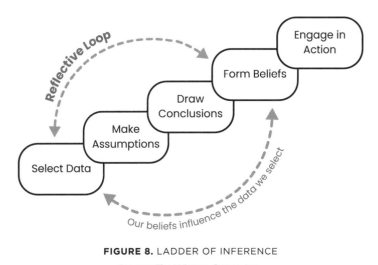

FIGURE 8. LADDER OF INFERENCE

Source: The Winters Group, Inc.,
adapted from *The Fifth Discipline Fieldbook* by Peter M. Senge,
Art Kleiner, Charlotte Roberts, Richard B. Ross, and Bryan J. Smith

system is based on a complex web of socioeconomic, historic, and race-based reasons.

If Jake believes interpretation #1, he will have little empathy and the polarization will continue. If Jake or Rodney believe interpretation #2 only, polarization is also likely to continue. (Remember the danger of a single story, discussed in Chapter 2.) Interpretation #3 is a much broader perspective, which allows Jake and Rodney to continue to dig deeper and expand their mutual understanding.

Here is how a shared-meaning dialogue might start.

JAKE: Based on what we've talked about, where do you think we are? I would like to think that we have created some shared understanding of the situation.

RODNEY: I think we have to some degree.

JAKE: Let's see if we can identify those areas of agreement and where we still have some opportunities.

RODNEY: Sounds good.

ARE YOU READY TO GET TO SHARED MEANING?
(A self-assessment)

◆ What am I feeling right now and why?

◆ Why did this event induce this particular reaction?

◆ Am I able to see the situation from all sides or am I looking at it in a polarized way?

◆ Do I realize that these situations are complex and not necessarily easily resolved?

◆ Am I expecting too much from my coworkers, colleagues, and friends?

◆ Do I have a trusted adviser/friend/confidant with whom I can be open and authentic?

◆ Am I fixed in my opinions or am I willing to learn how it might feel from the perspective of the other?

◆ What energy do I have to expend to learn more about the situation from the perspective of the other?

◆ Am I willing to put in the time that it will take?

◆ Am I willing to admit that I have biases and blind spots that may be getting in the way of my judgments?

◆ Am I willing to cut my coworkers some slack if they don't seem to understand?

◆ Can I live with the fact that some people really just may not care the way I do?

◆ Can I live with the fact that I may not be able to make them care?

◆ Am I willing to be patient and recognize that it may take some time and many teachable moments for my coworkers to understand my perspective?

◆ Am I prepared for, and comfortable with, agreeing to disagree?

Some potential areas of agreement for Jake and Rodney:

- We all want to be safe.
- We all want to be able to trust those in charge of keeping us safe.
- Historically, African Americans have had very different experiences than white people, and there is a need to foster deeper understanding of these differences.
- African Americans have spoken and unspoken concerns about the killing of unarmed Black men.
- These types of stresses can impact engagement and productivity.
- We don't know what we don't know, and we all have a lot to learn about each other to have effective dialogue.

At this juncture, these agreements are fairly noncontroversial. Even though Jake and Rodney have reached some level of agreement, they may still have some differing interpretations (e.g., how Jake interprets the concept of safety may be very different from how Rodney interprets it). For example, Jake has likely never thought about his safety on the metro track, as the gay, Muslim, Middle Eastern employee mentioned in Chapter 1 has. In other words, Jake may not connect safety with his identity as a white male.

Reflect and Learn More

Many stories matter. Stories have been used to dispossess and to malign, but stories can also be used to empower and to humanize. Stories can break the dignity of a people, but stories can also repair that broken dignity.

Chimamanda Ngozi Adichie [67]

After each conversation, you must take a learning and reflection period before the next encounter. At this juncture, each party has had an opportunity to be heard. You must now assess whether you need more listening to achieve shared meaning or if you can venture deeper in discussing your differences.

INTEGRATE BOLD, INCLUSIVE CONVERSATIONS INTO EXISTING PROCESSES

The process of getting to shared meaning should not be taken lightly. It may take several conversations and opportunities to learn and reflect to attain this goal. There is no set number of conversations to achieve shared meaning. It could take one or ten or more, for that matter. It depends on a number of different factors such as the topic, openness to accepting each other's perspective, the amount of new information that needs processing and understanding, and your willingness to continue given the emotional labor involved. You will have to learn to be comfortable with nonclosure. You may never get to closure, because this is a process—a journey, not a destination.

You might be thinking, we have an organization to run. We really don't have time for all of these side conversations that have nothing to do with our real work. However, an integral part of "real work" in today's workplace is fostering inclusion, which involves understanding our differences and how they can impact our sense of belonging and consequently our engagement.

Consider allocating some time for additional conversations as a part of weekly one-one's or team sessions that already take place during your normal operational processes. For example, if you typically have a one-hour one-one for work updates, incorporate the continued conversation into that time. If you have a cross-cultural learning program, as discussed in Chapter 3, or reciprocal mentoring, make it a part of that process. In other words, try to incorporate Bold, Inclusive Conversations into existing structures.

Let's assume that Rodney and Jake have achieved enough shared meaning that they are now ready for the next conversation, which will focus on their differences. We explore delving into differences in Chapter 6.

CHAPTER 5 ◆ TIPS FOR TALKING ABOUT IT!

◆ Plan to have several conversations that build on one another to reach the desired outcome of shared meaning and the ability to deeply understand each other's perspectives.

◆ Bold, Inclusive Conversations can be emotionally draining and even traumatizing. Set your own boundaries for how long and how much you will share in each session.

◆ Foster your ability to listen; it is the most important skill during the initial conversation.

◆ Schedule and plan for the conversation. Avoid spontaneous dialogues.

◆ If you are the initiator of the conversation, be prepared to share your perspectives based on the facts and your lived experiences.

◆ If you are not the initiator of the conversation, be prepared to just listen, and only ask questions for clarification.

◆ Engage in dialogue, not debate.

◆ Plan to reflect and engage in additional learning before the next conversation.

◆ If you were primarily listening during the first conversation, be prepared to share your perspective and ask questions during the second conversation.

- If you were the original convener, prepare to listen during the second conversation. Be patient with potential mistakes and misinformation. Be prepared to clarify points without judgment.

- Strive for shared meaning during the second conversation. Utilize the Ladder of Inference and the DNA model to reach mutual understanding.

- Keep in mind that there is no set number of conversations that will get you to shared meaning. It could be one or ten or more.

- Integrate Bold, Inclusive Conversations as a part of your normal one-one or team discussions.

SIX

◆ ◆ ◆

Let the Conversations Continue! Interpret and Bridge Differences

Tell the story of the mountains you climbed.
Your words could become a page in
someone else's survival guide.

MORGAN HARPER NICHOLS

Jake and Rodney are now ready for their third conversation, to delve into their different perspectives. Readiness to delve into differences may happen by the third conversation or it may not. It could happen before, depending on the readiness and preparation of each party as shown in our model for Bold, Inclusive Conversations.

It is hard to say how you will know when you are ready, but you will feel greater mutual understanding. You will recognize that you have amassed sufficient information about the other person or cultural group. You will sense that you are at a different place—a shift has occurred—and your worldview has changed from when you started the first conversation. Use the Am I Ready? guide (Guide 1) for determining when you might be ready for deeper conversations around polarizing topics.

GUIDE 1. AM I READY?

Readiness Level	Get Ready	Prepare	Converse	Primary Goal
New at This (*have not had bold, inclusive conversations*)	Focus mostly on self-understanding and other understanding. (Chapters 2–3).	Make sure you are prepared (Chapter 4).	Listen, learn, clarify, and reflect. Be patient. Build trust.	Listen in order to come to shared meaning.
Some Experience (*have had a few conversations*)	Focus mostly on other understanding (Chapter 3). This level assumes you have experience with at least one or two cultures other than your own.	Reflect on lessons learned from previous sessions. What would you do differently?	Listen, learn, and reflect. Question, clarify, and share your perspective. Be patient. Build trust.	Deeply explore differences.
Very Experienced	Focus mostly on exploring differences.	Reflect on lessons learned from previous sessions. What would you do differently?	Listen, learn, and reflect. Question, clarify, and share your perspective. Share deep personal stories. Be vulnerable. Share points of disagreement. Discuss ways to bridge differences to achieve a win-win. Trust level should already be high.	Bridge cultural differences. Strive for reciprocal empathy.

ACKNOWLEDGE THE ELEPHANT IN THE ROOM

Delving into differences is the most difficult part of the conversation process. Acknowledging that polarized opinions exist is the first step.

Continuing with our story of Rodney and Jake, let's look at the polarization that they might acknowledge now. According to many research studies, Blacks and whites differ significantly on their views of racial issues. For example, a 2022 Pew Research Center study showed that Blacks, Latines, and Asians were much more likely to support the Black Lives Matter movement than whites, as Figure 9 shows. Notably, Black respondents were almost twice as likely to support the Black Lives Matter movement as whites.[68]

In another Pew Research Center study conducted in 2021, 75 percent of Black respondents said that the increased attention on the history of slavery and racism is very good or good for society, whereas only 46 percent of white respondents answered similarly.[69]

The reflection and learning that Jake and Rodney have engaged in up to this point should have already surfaced some of the reasons for polarization on these issues. Therefore, both Jake and Rodney should be armed with more knowledge. That does not necessarily mean that they have each shifted toward completely agreeing with the other's perspective.

They had to come to some shared understanding, including wanting all of our children to be safe. Jake may still have a hard time believing that the police actually profile a certain race for no legitimate reason, and Rodney still may believe that Jake's white privilege keeps him from seeing the full picture. Dialoguing rather than debating as described in Chapter 5 is particularly important at this stage of the process.

Continuing with Jake and Rodney's conversations from

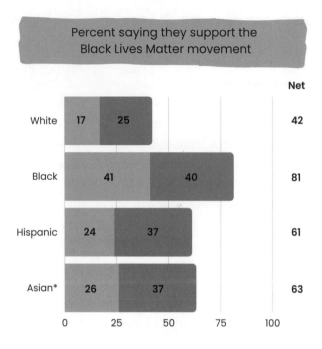

FIGURE 9. SUPPORT FOR BLACK LIVES MATTER MOVEMENT
BY RACE/ETHNICITY

Source: The Winters Group, Inc., adapted from Pew Research Center

Chapter 5, their third conversation might start with something like this:

JAKE: I have been reading a lot about how Blacks are treated in the criminal justice system. I really had no idea of the disparities. It looks like the reasons are fairly complex.

RODNEY: They are. Do you agree that the disparities are largely due to discrimination?

JAKE: I'm not sure. I always thought that our justice system was pretty color blind. If you do the crime you pay your time, so to speak.

RODNEY (rephrasing rather than defending at this point): So, what I hear you saying is that you think the system is fair.

JAKE: Yes, for the most part, I think so, or at least I thought so. The stats do show that Blacks commit more crimes than whites.

RODNEY: That does not necessarily mean that the system is fair. It's also true that Blacks are 7.5 times more likely to be wrongly convicted and later exonerated of criminal charges.[70]

DISTINGUISH DIFFERENT INTERPRETATIONS AND CLARIFY DEFINITIONS

Let's consider the interpretation of fairness. Fairness to Jake might look like the rules are applied the same to everybody regardless of race (minimization worldview, described in Chapter 3). He may envision a meritocracy.

For Rodney, fairness may be less fixed and depend on circumstances. Rodney might think that it is important to address past wrongs in determining what is fair.

To have meaningful conversations about difference, we should define and clarify terms. If there are different interpretations, keep them visible (perhaps on chart paper or captured on a projection device). At this juncture, do not debate the validity of the different definitions; simply acknowledge and make note of them.

UNCOVER YOUR DIFFERENT PERSPECTIVES

When we embrace a polarization mindset, we typically have a very simplistic understanding of our differences. However, if we have gone through the 4-E steps to broaden our knowledge, we have likely moved to minimization, where we can focus on similarities and shared values. At this orientation on the Intercultural Development Continuum (see Chapter 3), we may be able to move from overemphasizing our similarities to accepting that there are differences that make a difference in how we are treated. We become more curious and open-minded.

At this juncture, the conversation may go something like this:

JAKE: While I am disturbed by the disproportionality in the statistics showing the number of incarcerated Blacks, the facts also show that Blacks perpetuate more violent crimes, overall, and much of it is Black-on-Black crime, isn't it?

RODNEY: Yes, it is, but the numbers are similar for white-on-white crime. For example, I found that according to FBI statistics, 81 percent of white victims were killed by white offenders, and 89 percent of Black victims were killed by Black offenders.[71]

JAKE: Well, I guess statistics can be deceiving if you don't have the full story. I'm glad we're able to discuss this really difficult topic. It gives me more to think about.

RODNEY: I'm happy too that you're willing to be curious and try to better understand the complexities of race and racism in this country.

JAKE: I am sure that I still have a lot to learn, and I'd like to continue the conversation so that you can help me.

RODNEY: While I'm happy to support you, I think it's important that you not just rely on me and take the initiative to do your own work. There are many great resources to help you in your journey.

JAKE: I will certainly do that. I really think life is what we make it in the end. People can make lemonade out of lemons, you know. There are a lot of stories about how you people have overcome the odds. I don't understand why more of you people don't. You made it.

Rodney felt a bit surprised by Jake's "pull yourself up by your bootstraps" assertion and realized that he was getting frustrated and somewhat angry. He felt himself about to lose it when Jake said "you people." Jake probably did not know why those two words were triggering for Rodney (see Chapter 8 for an explanation). Remembering his emotional intelligence skills, Rodney knew he needed to manage his feelings at that point. He did not want to show Jake how frustrated he had become. Rather than continue the conversation, Rodney chose to pause it. He had started to feel the emotional toll that can manifest during Bold, Inclusive Conversations. It is important for Rodney to be self-aware and attend to his own well-being.

RODNEY (IN A NEUTRAL TONE): While I did succeed, every person's circumstance is different. I think we've gone far enough with this topic today. I would like to give you some additional information that might help broaden your understanding. I would also like to suggest that during our next conversation we talk about our respective life experiences. I want you to know more about who I am, my experiences, and I would like to know the same about you.

JAKE: Yes, I would like that too. Let's plan on it.

KNOW WHEN TO PUT THE CONVERSATION ON PAUSE

Bold, Inclusive Conversations can be emotionally draining and sometimes harmful to our well-being. It is important to consider the emotional toll. We should advocate for setting boundaries that help the individuals engaged in these conversations to protect their mental and emotional health.

It would have been futile for Rodney and Jake to continue their conversation. Stopping and agreeing to do some more reflection and learning, and to come back later to continue, made sense for Rodney's well-being. When we deadlock around ideologies, emotions may run high, and we might sink back into polarization. There may also be instances where the perspectives are just so different that they create a permanent impasse and further discussion becomes unuseful. When that happens, we must consider whether we can accept another's perspective even when we don't agree and whether doing so will harm us or others. We should also consider the nature of the relationship between the individuals. In this instance, Jake is Rodney's boss. What impact might such differences have on their working relationship? If Rodney believes that Jake's positions are potentially harmful, he may have to think about his ability to continue to work with Jake.

TELL YOUR STORY

The truth is, reflection is tough work because it requires that we all take responsibility in creating the future we want.
Shawn A. Ginwright[72]

When Jake and Rodney come back together for their fourth conversation, they have agreed to tell their stories. Storytelling is a very powerful learning tool. Everybody has a diversity story, regardless of their race, gender, or sexual orientation.

However, we must be ready to hear someone else's story in a way that will have a compelling impact and foster greater understanding.

Telling stories when the parties remain polarized can move them deeper into polarization, because at this stage, they are each wedded to their own opinion and may consider the other's story an excuse, an exaggeration, or not relevant to the facts; they may use such rationales to deny the validity of the other's story. Conversely, storytelling could have a positive outcome—an epiphany that moves individuals out of polarization to a place of greater understanding.

We have seen it work both ways. In one situation, after a compelling story from an African American woman who felt labeled as an angry Black woman, one of her white female colleagues said, "I don't think that has anything to do with race at all. I could say the same label happens for white women." It effectively invalidated the African American woman's story.

On the other hand, the story of the gay Muslim man who would not stand close to the edge of the metro platform, referenced earlier, provided an aha experience for one of his white senior leaders, who was shocked that anyone would carry such a fear with them every day.

Rodney and Jake have not yet shared their deep personal stories. They have pretty much stayed at the cognitive level of facts and logic. Jake has a discussion style orientation (as assessed by the Intercultural Conflict Style Inventory discussed in Chapter 3) and he therefore found it appropriate to provide a more logical, fact-based argument, rather than use the engagement style more associated with personal story telling. The time has come for them to have a conversation about their life experiences and how these experiences have shaped them.

There are pros and cons to placing this type of sharing

at this point in the process, rather than during the first two conversations structured around listening. The advantage of storytelling early on is that it fosters openness and transparency, which can build trust and empathy and may lead to transformative aha moments early on that can result in delving into differences sooner. The drawback is there may not be enough mutual trust that early in the process for the parties to feel comfortable sharing at this deep level. One of the primary purposes of the early conversations is to build trust.

If there is adequate readiness early in the process, based on the self-assessment in Chapter 3, sharing stories can be quite impactful during the listening phase.

WHERE DO JAKE AND RODNEY GO FROM HERE?

What's next for Jake and Rodney after they share their respective stories in their fourth conversation? They need to keep chipping away at more mutual understanding, which does not necessarily mean agreement or consensus. Perhaps they incorporate further conversations into their regular one-one meetings, as recommended in Chapter 5. They may find some topics where they agree to disagree while still respecting each other's right to have a different point of view. Keeping boundaries in mind, if a point of view is harmful to others, it should not be respected. Diversity, equity, and inclusion is not a neutral topic. It advocates for fairness and righting past wrongs to achieve an equitable society. For example, legislation that bans books about race and racism and efforts to eliminate diversity offices in public higher education harms us all. We are deprived of learning about our history and continuing efforts to right past wrongs. Bold, Inclusive Conversations are only possible when the parties can reach common ground on fundamental issues, such as structural racism, religious freedom, and women's reproductive health.

Rodney and Jake now both have a greater capacity to have Bold, Inclusive Conversations. They have done the hard readiness work recommended in Chapters 2 and 3 and have had some breakthrough conversations that shifted perspectives. They have enhanced their level of trust so that if they want to discuss another polarizing topic, they are not starting from scratch. They may need to repeat some of the readiness steps to learn about a new topic, but they may be able to delve into their differences much faster.

Rodney had initially requested a team meeting to discuss his concerns about the killings of unarmed Black men. Jake is in a much better position now to make a decision about the advisability of such a session. Rodney, too, has a better vantage point. They decide that Jake will allocate one of their team meetings to share what he has learned, stressing the importance of supporting each other during times of trauma. This will be an opportunity for the team to listen to Jake as the leader and for Jake to answer questions other employees might have. Depending on the interest and readiness of the team, Jake will decide if additional conversations should take place. In addition, Rodney will seek support from the Black employee network group, where he can commiserate with others who may share his fears and anxieties.

THE END POINT:
RECIPROCAL EMPATHY

If there is an endpoint to Bold, Inclusive Conversations, it is reciprocal empathy (i.e., the ability to know what it is like to be the other). If we can get to that point, we increase the likelihood of generating new ways to engage with each other.

We have learned more about our similarities and differences; we have built better relationships and improved trust. Employees will feel more valued and respected and will be more motivated to give their all. This in turn leads to greater productivity, engagement, and innovation. One of the participants from one of the dialogue sessions outlined in Chapter 1 summed it up this way: "I will go back to work now knowing that others are feeling like I do. Just being able to openly talk about it makes me feel better, and I can go back to giving my all. Somebody understands."

CELEBRATE LITTLE BREAKTHROUGHS AND KEEP PRACTICING

We keep reiterating that this is a process, one that has no specific ending. Learning how to have Bold, Inclusive Conversations is a journey, not a destination. You have to keep chipping away at it a little bit at a time, just like any other competency. If you are learning to play the piano, you keep practicing until you are able to play more difficult pieces. Actually, to keep the skill, you will never stop practicing. And so it is with Bold, Inclusive Conversations.

CHAPTER 6 ◆ TIPS FOR TALKING ABOUT IT!

- ◆ Recognize that it is hard to predict when you will be ready to delve into deep, polarizing differences. You will have felt some type of shift in your worldview perspective.

- ◆ Acknowledge the points of polarization at the beginning of the conversation to attempt to achieve common ground.

- ◆ Clarify meanings and interpretations. Allow for multiple interpretations as you sort out your different perspectives.

- ◆ When you reach an impasse put the conversation on pause.

- ◆ Set boundaries to protect your mental well-being. Learn to manage your emotions when there is disagreement.

◆ Sharing your story is a very powerful way to foster understanding. You must build some level of trust for your story to be understood and validated.

◆ Recognize that there is no real end point to Bold, Inclusive Conversations as this is a journey not a destination. You keep developing and learning.

◆ Seek reciprocal empathy.

◆ Celebrate the little breakthroughs as much as the big wins.

SEVEN

Actualizing Bold, Inclusive Conversations at Work

The Engaging in Bold, Inclusive Conversations Facilitator Certification Program is impressive at equipping organizations to effectively manage polarizing topics that are potentially disengaging our employees. We can no longer ignore the reality that these conversations are happening in the workplace. This program gives us proven strategies to bridge different realities to build stronger working relationships.

ENGAGING IN BOLD, INCLUSIVE CONVERSATIONS
FACILITATOR CERTIFICATION PROGRAM PARTICIPANT

After the release of the first edition of this book, we developed a facilitator certification program grounded in the model for Bold, Inclusive Conversations. Because it takes a unique skill to facilitate conversations about race, religion, politics, and other polarizing topics, we wanted to provide a training program to support organizations in having effective dialogue. The Facilitator Certification Program is a three-day, interactive, skill-building learning experience that provides participants with content, tools, and competencies necessary to strengthen their and their organization's capacity to engage in Bold, Inclusive Conversations.

In this chapter, we share ways to actualize Bold, Inclusive

Conversations at work by integrating this content into existing training programs. We will also provide our method for
preparing facilitators to deliver the content. At the end of the
chapter, we highlight two organizations that have had several
cohorts of employees matriculate through the Engaging in
Bold, Inclusive Conversations Facilitator Certification Program and how they have successfully incorporated our model
into their overall DEI strategy.

EQUIPPING ORGANIZATIONS WITH SKILLS TO ENGAGE IN BOLD, INCLUSIVE CONVERSATIONS

Our Engaging in Bold, Inclusive Conversations Facilitator
Certification Program is not a check the box program; nor
is it intended to be a deep dive on specific diversity topics. It
offers a starting point for understanding and developing the
skills and competencies required to engage in Bold, Inclusive Conversations. Through the program, participants have
access to predesigned, licensed learning experiences that
can be leveraged internally in their organizations to equip
learners with the skills and competencies required to engage
in Bold, Inclusive Conversations at work. For example, it
includes a video rendition of the Jake and Rodney conversation outlined in Chapters 5 and 6.

Throughout the three days, participants:

◆ **Learn** the content, tools, and competencies necessary to
strengthen their capacity to facilitate and engage in Bold,
Inclusive Conversations.

◆ **Understand** the model for engaging in Bold, Inclusive
Conversations as outlined in this book.

◆ **Explore** the sociopolitical climate and its impact on the
workplace.

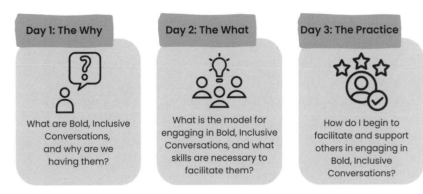

FIGURE 10. ENGAGING IN BOLD, INCLUSIVE CONVERSATIONS
FACILITATOR CERTIFICATION PROGRAM OVERVIEW

- ◆ **Enhance** facilitation skills necessary for cross-cultural conversations and polarizing topics.
- ◆ **Enhance** their self-understanding and awareness of potential obstruction spots that might impede their effectiveness as a facilitator.
- ◆ **Connect** the learning to organizational objectives (e.g., "bring your whole self to work," engage with empathy, create an inclusive culture).
- ◆ **Practice** facilitating Bold, Inclusive Conversations learning content.

LEARNING TO FACILITATE POLARIZING TOPICS

We support participants in building the skills to facilitate polarizing topics. As prework, participants complete the Intercultural Development Inventory (see Chapter 2) and the Intercultural Conflict Style Inventory (see Chapter 3) to assess their ability to bridge across differences, and their culturally informed conflict style. Self-awareness is critical in developing facilitation skills. Recognizing their worldview orientation toward difference as measured by the Intercultural Development Inventory supports participants in better understanding their individual developmental opportunities to enhance their cultural competence. Discussing polarizing topics can lead to conflict; therefore, being aware of their own conflict style and that of others can help facilitators manage Bold, Inclusive Conversations more effectively. On the third day of the program (as shown in Figure 10) participants practice facilitating Bold, Inclusive Conversations content through an exercise called Teach Backs. They gain comfort in how to convey the concepts outlined in this book.

An important first step during an education experience around Bold, Inclusive Conversations is establishing ground rules or norms that all participants agree to and hold each other accountable to as part of the session. As a facilitator you may choose to identify community norms as a group activity, or you may already have some norms established. Examples of some norms or agreements include:

◆ Centering the experiences of those most impacted.

◆ Choosing curiosity over judgment.

◆ Modeling authenticity and vulnerability.

◆ Recognizing the limitation of your own lens.

◆ Stating your intentions and owning your impact.

◆ Speaking from the "I" and not the "we."

You may need to distinguish interpretations and clarify definitions of these norms (or other terms within the session). Even "universal" terms and values can be interpreted differently across cultures. What do terms like *fairness, safety,* and *trust* mean to those involved in the dialogue? Discuss those differences. You might ask: "I heard you mention earlier that we all want to feel heard and respected—but what does respect look like for you? What are some of the behaviors you associate with respect?"

There will obviously be diverse perspectives in sessions where polarizing topics are discussed. During the certification program we provide advice on how to facilitate such situations. For example, if a conversation about religion surfaces differing opinions, a facilitator might say the following: "I want to recognize and name the many different perspectives on the topic of religion here. Some believe there is no place in the workplace for these discussions, but our organization's commitment to inclusion requires that we lean into these topics. I invite you to listen with curiosity. We are not attempting to change anyone's beliefs but rather to understand how we can support the different needs of our employees in an inclusive way."

MOVING BEYOND NEUTRALITY

If you are neutral in situations of injustice, you have chosen the side of the oppressor. If an elephant has its foot on the tail of a mouse, and you say that you are neutral, the mouse will not appreciate your neutrality.

Desmond Tutu[73]

As a facilitator, you may have a different viewpoint than those who are participating in your session. How do you navigate this? Should you strive to be neutral? Reflect on the quote above by Desmond Tutu. What does it evoke for you? When thinking about DEI work, is remaining neutral the goal? We think it is not. Equity requires us to consider historical insult, providing what people need to level the playing field. This requires moving beyond neutrality to centering those most impacted.

The goal for any dialogue should be to allow individuals to walk away with new insights and perspectives and to create opportunities for shared meaning/common ground. In the context of polarizing topics, the goal should be to bring historically marginalized perspectives to the center for consideration. **Multipartiality** is a practice to get us there; it supports facilitators in giving equal attention to multiple identities and experiences. Most importantly, it supports facilitators in giving attention to those identities and experiences that might be absent or unheard. As facilitators, we may be more partial to our points of views or perhaps those of others that jibe with our own. Multipartiality means that we include the most needed, unheard, undervalued voices as well.

Practicing multipartiality means that we:

+ Identify the goal: "The goal of this conversation is to..."
+ Discourage binaries by using "both/and..." instead of narratives or arguments that suggest "either/or."
+ Call out the gaps by asking, "Who is not a part of this conversation [or community, group]? Why?"
+ Redirect from dominant narratives by asking, "Does anyone have a different experience from those shared?"
+ Be prepared to share unrepresented experiences using narrative, video, guest speakers, and so on.
+ Clarify what is at stake: "If we do not consider the experiences of [underrepresented group], then..."
+ Be mindful of emotional labor.

As a facilitator it is also important to manage your emotions. Participants may express perspectives that are contrary to your beliefs or the beliefs of others in the room that could be triggering or evoke negative emotions. The following tips from Leigh Morrison of The Winters Group can help with preemptively managing triggers while facilitating training sessions on polarizing topics:[74]

- **Spend time reflecting on topics that are triggering for you and likely to bring you to an emotionally charged place.** Make a list of times you recall becoming emotional about equity and inclusion topics, whether facilitating, having a conversation with someone, or consuming media. Consider writing or talking about these topics to process them further and lessen the intensity of your response in the future.

- **Prepare and practice responses to common microaggressions.** If you practice explaining a topic, it will come to mind more easily in the midst of an emotionally challenging situation. (See the list of common microaggressions in Chapter 8.)

- **Consider what dominant group memberships you hold and how to use them to relate to individuals who express challenging statements.** Practice this internally to promote empathy (*I used to feel similarly about this/ another topic before I learned more about it; how can I help this person to shift their perspective?*) or externally to find common ground ("I was raised to think that too. Through interacting more with people from that group, I have come to realize why that isn't the whole story."). Reflect upon and practice sharing examples from your own experiences so that these are salient when you need them.

- **Pause the conversation during emotionally charged situations.** Remember the conversation between Rodney and Jake in Chapter 6. They needed to pause and reflect before resuming their discussion. Consider naming some of the dynamics you are tracking ("I am sensing that this topic may be emotional for some people in the room. Let's pause for a moment to check in with ourselves."). Ask participants to take a few deep breaths or otherwise ground themselves and use this as an opportunity to "reset" and consider the best response.

◆ **Lean on the support and knowledge of others in the room.** If you are fortunate enough to be facilitating with another person, discuss ahead of time how you can communicate a need to "take a step back," and let them step in to manage the conversation while you collect your thoughts. If you are the only facilitator, you can ask the group about their thoughts. "What do others think about that?" and "Does anyone have a different perspective?" are two questions that can both leverage participants' knowledge and give you a moment to breathe.

◆ **Rather than responding directly to a shared statement, consider how you could ask the person to clarify their perspective or challenge them to think further.** This is a key facilitation skill; it also has the added benefit of taking some pressure off and giving you a moment to reflect rather than responding with the first emotionally charged thought that comes to your mind.

While it may be our goal as practitioners and facilitators to be "on" at all times, we are all humans with identities, experiences, and emotions that complicate this goal. We can and should honor this truth, in service to ourselves and our learners.

ASSESSING YOUR ORGANIZATION'S READINESS TO INCORPORATE BOLD, INCLUSIVE CONVERSATIONS

We encourage you to make developing the skills, strategies, and competencies for Bold, Inclusive Conversations part of your organization's learning strategy. We are often asked where this type of learning falls within an organization's broader DEI curriculum. As discussed in Chapters 2

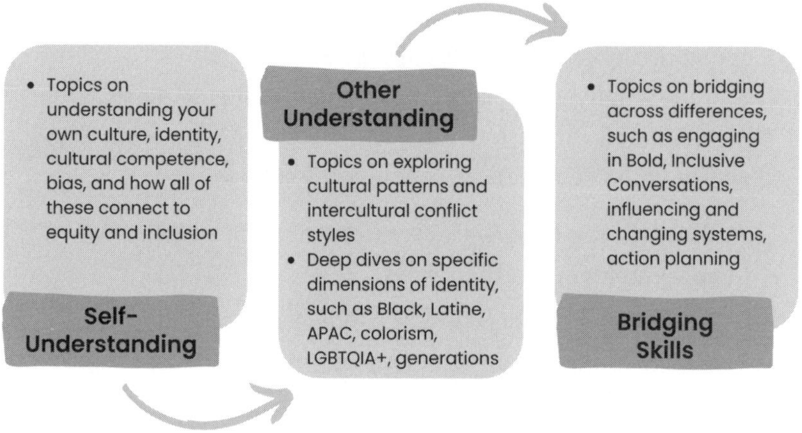

FIGURE 11. SELF–OTHER–BRIDGING MODEL

and 3, the first steps to Bold, Inclusive Conversations are self- and other understanding. This aligns with The Winters Group's approach to learning. Successful DEI learning begins with foundational knowledge and self-understanding, then progresses into understanding of the other, and culminates with skills to bridge across differences. In Figure 11 we offer our Self–Other–Bridging learning model to show what a developmental DEI curriculum that includes Bold, Inclusive Conversations content might look like. The Bold, Inclusive Conversations content is about bridging skills, assuming that curriculum is in place that addresses self- and other under-standing. We do not recommend engaging in this learning without foundation building around diversity, equity, and inclusion topics, as it could potentially further polarize.

In Chapter 2 we also discuss organizational readiness as a prerequisite to engaging in Bold, Inclusive Conversations. Prior to rolling out Bold, Inclusive Conversations learn-ing, take the organizational readiness assessment outlined in Chapter 3. Your responses may inform the learning that needs to take place in self- and other understanding, prior to engaging in bridging skills content.

Additionally, when thinking about who should participate in facilitated education on Bold, Inclusive Conversations within your organization, consider the following:

◆ How will the Bold, Inclusive Conversations model support employees in their roles?

◆ In what ways is this content connected to specific goals, responsibilities, competencies, or objectives?

◆ What DEI-related education have the employees already experienced?

◆ What is their level of engagement and/or buy-in around these topics?

REAL-LIFE ORGANIZATIONS SUCCESSFULLY USING THE BOLD, INCLUSIVE CONVERSATIONS MODEL

Participants of our Facilitator Certification Program come from both the nonprofit and for-profit sectors. We have worked with organizations in various industries, such as health care, government, education (K–12 and higher education), technology, and professional services, just to name a few. Our content for building the capacity to have difficult conversations around polarizing topics is applicable for all industries and all levels within organizations.

We interviewed two organizations who have participated in private sessions of our Facilitator Certification Program to equip their staff with the skills to facilitate learning experiences based on the Bold, Inclusive Conversations model. Below we highlight their experiences thus far to support you as you consider incorporating this work into your own organization.

Merck

It is important to be talking about polarizing topics at work because the workplace is an engine of well-being. We spend so much of our daily lives working with colleagues with diverse backgrounds and beliefs, [therefore] we have the most opportunities at work to build our confidence and capability to have difficult conversations in the workplace.

Christopher Cardarelli, Executive Director, Global
Diversity and Inclusion, Merck[75]

Merck has demonstrated a commitment to diversity and inclusion for many years. They recognize that diversity and inclusion are critical to their ability to deliver on their purpose of using the power of leading-edge science to save and improve lives around the world. Merck's D&I strategy includes global diversity and inclusion (GD&I) learning and development programs, GD&I ambassador teams, and employee business resource groups (EBRGs). Merck strives to create an environment where all employees feel safe to speak up and belong. As a component of Merck's GD&I learning and development program offerings, they have incorporated education on Bold, Inclusive Conversations, demonstrating their commitment to creating a safe space for employees to thrive.[76]

Merck has certified twenty-one facilitators through our Engaging in Bold, Inclusive Conversations Facilitator Certification Program. Using The Winters Group licensed content, they have delivered training globally across the organization, reaching over three thousand employees. When participants were queried on what gets in the way of engaging in Bold, Inclusive Conversations in the workplace, most shared fear and the lack of education. Merck's goal with this learning experience is to build both confidence *and* competence in having Bold, Inclusive Conversations across the organization. Participants give high marks on applying the program to the job; shifting behaviors in how they show up at work; delivering value for themselves and others; and benefiting from the overall experience.

As a component of the divisions' DEI strategy, Merck delivers this content through (1) open enrollment sessions, and (2) targeted sessions for specific business areas or teams. Because of the COVID-19 pandemic, learning has been delivered virtually, and they find this to actually be "more inclusive" than in-person sessions due to the ability to reach more people globally. In some areas, they rolled out the learning in phases by level within the organization, starting with leaders/managers and moving down to individual contributors.

Another way Merck is building internal capacity is by having business-unit specific certified facilitators. These individuals sit outside of HR and directly support site-level business leaders who have identified the business need for building skill and capability among managers and teams.

Outside of the formal program, Merck's HR team has embedded aspects of the Bold, Inclusive Conversations model into leadership coaching, especially the 4-Es (see Chapter 3). They have found that the 4-E framework creates a backdrop for reflection, especially when giving/receiving feedback.

Merck delivers sessions to global audiences, and facilitators are mindful to leverage examples that extend beyond just a US lens to connect with a global audience, using examples such as gender, LGBTQIA+, religion, and politics. While race is not strictly a US phenomenon, using more familiar language and regional/local examples has helped to ensure concepts resonate.

As a pharmaceutical company, Merck emphasizes the importance of safety at work. The safety of employees is not just about physical safety; it is inclusive of emotional and psychological safety as well. Educating employees on the

Bold, Inclusive Conversations model allows Merck to deliver the message of safety more holistically. Merck is creating a safer place for employees by building their capacity to engage in conversations around topics that are polarizing and once considered taboo.

Organization X
(A Government Services Organization)

The truth of the matter is these conversations around these topics are not going to get easier. It's getting harder and harder, so we are going to have to find ways to be able to engage in a way so that we invite people into the conversation instead of alienating them from the conversations.

Senior Leader, Organization X

The Winters Group has facilitated five private Engaging in Bold, Inclusive Conversations Facilitator Certification Programs for a government services organization, hereinafter referred to as Organization X. Organization X is using the program and the Bold, Inclusive Conversations model as a preparation tool for their in-house facilitators. These facilitators teach many courses, including courses on various diversity, equity, and inclusion topics. Beyond equipping these facilitators with the skills and competencies to facilitate content around Bold, Inclusive Conversations, Organization X is also preparing them to model the framework for all types of conversations, such as team meetings. The goal is to expand the role/responsibility beyond that of DEI facilitator to "DEI champions" who help others navigate through diversity, equity, and inclusion work and difficult conversations.

For the existing DEI courses, they have relied on the Bold, Inclusive Conversations model and related content as the foundation, particularly as the external sociopolitical climate continues to rapidly change. They have found that the model

offers the skills and competencies needed to navigate conversations. Organization X has incorporated content from
the Facilitator Certification Program into existing DEI foundational courses and will be rolling out full Bold, Inclusive
Conversations content to the organization in the future as
part of their broader learning strategy.

The biggest success that Organization X has found with
the Bold, Inclusive Conversations model is the ability to better navigate conversations that had previously been difficult
by enhancing psychological safety. Additionally, it has provided the organization's facilitators with a toolkit for how to
approach various issues that may come up during training
sessions. Facilitators have gained a lens to look at other situations and level the playing field in terms of equity in how to
communicate, how to conduct meetings, and how to interact
with one another and enter a virtual space. The Bold, Inclusive Conversations model and the tools and competencies
learned in the Facilitator Certification Program have helped
Organization X's facilitators recognize microaggressions that
might occur in different environments and situations, and
how to address them.

One of the greatest hurdles for Organization X has been
dialoguing around issues that have become politicized. The
political and apolitical are no longer clearly defined, and as
the lines become blurred, Organization X recognizes the
need to be mindful about how to navigate conversations that
on the surface may seem benign from a political lens but,
depending on the conversation, may be received as having a
political slant. To address this, they ensure that the conversation is tied to the mission and values of the organization.

Organization X has found that younger generations joining the workforce expect and even demand more action by
organizations. They are more likely to require a higher level

of response when difficult external events occur. Therefore, Organization X thinks it is imperative to equip leaders and employees with the skills to engage in Bold, Inclusive Conversations and make it a part of their culture.

CHAPTER 7 ◆ TIPS FOR TALKING ABOUT IT!

◆ Prior to incorporating Bold, Inclusive Conversations in your organization's learning strategy, assess organizational readiness (see Chapter 3).

◆ Organizations that equip employees to have Bold, Inclusive Conversations do so to create more inclusive, psychologically safe environments.

◆ Organizations adapt the Bold, Inclusive Conversations model to be relevant for the topics and issues important in their regions of the world.

◆ When delivering content on Bold, Inclusive Conversations, establish ground rules or norms up front to allow participants to feel safe and brave in sessions.

◆ Understand that even topics that seem to be neutral or safe on the surface might be polarizing; therefore, it is important to be prepared to facilitate such discussions.

◆ Tie engaging in Bold, Inclusive Conversations to the overall organizational goals, mission, vision, and strategy.

EIGHT

Sharpen Inclusive Habits

Let your humanity shine through all you do. We may not fully agree with one another, but we can always act humanely toward one another.

MAREISHA N. REESE

The need for Bold, Inclusive Conversations on polarizing topics in the workplace will ebb and flow. The sociopolitical climate makes it imperative to be prepared for these types of conversations. This chapter provides guidance for honing inclusive habits that you will want to practice on a regular basis—even when not preparing for a Bold, Inclusive Conversation.

INCLUSIVE HABITS TO LIVE BY

We have found that these habits can enhance everyone's capacity for inclusion.

Acknowledging the limitations of your own lens. You don't know everything; there is always something to learn.

Validating: Others' perspectives are just as valid to them as yours are to you and should be listened to for understanding, not necessarily agreement.

Listening to understand. Listen for your own cultural assumptions, perceptions, and expectations.

Reflecting: Spend more time reflecting on your own values and beliefs. Why do you believe what you believe? Why would someone believe the opposite? Can you respect the beliefs of others even when you don't agree?

Describing: Learn to describe a behavior before providing your interpretation, and expand the number of interpretations you consider. Use the DNA model outlined in Chapter 2 to support this habit.

Contextualizing: Consider the circumstances, conditions, and history of the topics for which you are having Bold, Inclusive Conversations. Provide the proper context for each conversation.

Pausing before speaking to consider what you are feeling. Also know when to pause a conversation when you reach an impasse. Set boundaries that preserve everyone's well-being.

Accepting: Accepting does not mean agreeing. You can accept that there are myriad worldviews, and it is important to learn more about them. Accepting is better than tolerating. How do you feel when someone tells you that they will tolerate you? Not so good, right? Many diversity programs advocate for tolerance. Work to move from tolerance to acceptance. As mentioned in Chapter 6, there are boundaries to acceptance: if the perspective is harmful to others, you should not accept it. This may make it possible to find mutual ground.

Questioning: Show genuine interest in others. Be curious, not judgmental, about their experiences.

Respecting: Respect the humanity of every person even when you don't agree with them. Separate the person from the position if the position is not harmful to others. Practice the platinum rule by treating others the way they want to be treated.

Apologizing: What do you do when you make a mistake or say the wrong thing because you just did not know? As we suggest in Chapter 3, we have to learn to be patient of mistakes and cut each other some slack. If you say something that offends someone else, genuinely apologize. The impact on the other person may be very different from what you intended. Do not defend your comment. Simply say, "I am sorry. Please help me understand why that was offensive." Consider it an opportunity to learn, but do not expect the other person to be ready to share in the moment, if at all. Refer to the next section in this chapter for guidance on triggers and microinequities that different groups might find offensive.

Connecting: Making meaningful connections across difference is one sure way of breaking down barriers and enhancing our capacity for empathy and shared understanding.

Empathizing: Sympathy leads to patronization and pity. Empathy allows you to see the situation from the perspective of the other person.

TRIGGERS AND MICROINEQUITIES: BARRIERS TO BOLD, INCLUSIVE CONVERSATIONS

There are some key triggers that we should avoid in our attempts to be inclusive—words and phrases that may be considered offensive, derogatory, or insensitive by different identity groups. Sometimes referred to as **microinequities** or **microaggressions**, these seemingly small, offhand comments build up over time and erode trust and the possibility of meaningful conversations.

156   WE CAN'T TALK ABOUT THAT AT WORK!

Because we are individuals, these may not be triggers for all members of a particular identity. We are simply providing some examples to help you as you prepare for your Bold, Inclusive Conversations. This is not intended to be an exhaustive list. It is also not an attempt at "political correctness." Rather, we want to provide an understanding of why certain terms may be offensive. Do not try to memorize the list. Reflect on it to support you in advancing your cultural competence. What other examples might you add to the list?

These terms are more US centric because that is our lived experience. Therefore, they might not apply globally. For example, when we use the term *Americans*, we are referring to people living in the United States and its territories rather than the whole of North America or South America. You should research the ones applicable in your region of the world.

Black/African American People in the United States

The following are some key triggers for African Americans:

"You are so articulate." It suggests that the speaker is surprised and has a preconceived notion that Black people are less intelligent than white people.

"You people." This perpetuates the "us-and-them" mentality and suggests that the person addressed doesn't belong here. It also stereotypes by lumping all Black people together, implying they are all alike.

References to monkeys/apes. Black people have been compared to monkeys throughout history in a way that implies they are less human. For example, Michelle Obama was likened to apes and monkeys throughout her time as First Lady. Even the phrase "don't monkey around" can be a trigger.

"When I look at you, I don't see color." We have been taught that it is best to be color blind and just treat everybody the same. Color blindness negates the person's identity and their lived experience of moving through the world as a Black person.

"America is a melting pot." The melting pot analogy invalidates the person's unique identity and perpetuates the idea of sameness and assimilation. A more appropriate metaphor might be a stew, a symphony, or a salad, where the individual pieces remain visible.

"There is only one race—the human race." While from a biological perspective that might be true, race is an important social construct. We live in a racialized hierarchy where historically those identifying as white are on the top and those identifying as Black are on the bottom. This statement can be interpreted as denying the different experiences of people of color.

"I am not a racist. I have several Black friends." The speaker may not be a racist. However, the racial makeup of their group of friends does not determine whether their attitudes and behaviors are racist.

"I don't think that has/had anything to do with race." For a Black person, everything has something to do with race. The sheer fact of being visibly different makes it impossible to eliminate race from any interaction. If the Black person thinks that race plays a factor, then that perception is their truth. It is important to acknowledge, validate, and understand that perspective.

"As a woman, I know what you go through as a racial minority." This diminishes the uniqueness of the experience of the African American. While there may be similarities, a white woman's experience is not the same as an African

American's. It would be like saying, "I had breast cancer and you had colon cancer, so I understand your experience." There are likely similarities but also important differences to consider.

"We are looking to hire more BIPOC as long as they are qualified." Putting the caveat of "qualified" with "minorities" suggests that the speaker believes minorities are less qualified.

The label Angry Black Woman or Angry Black Man. There is a stereotype that Black people are an angry lot, especially Black women, though Black men are often depicted this way as well. A few years ago, I (Mary-Frances) offered my opinion on some aspects of diversity at a conference. Later, I heard that someone there wanted to meet me, or specifically, he wanted to meet the person who was "ranting." I was really taken aback. I knew I was passionate, but ranting? No way. I interpreted that as a very negative description. Generally speaking, African Americans are more direct and expressive in their communication style, which can often be confused as anger.

American Indians in the United States

For American Indians or Indigenous people of the United States, the following terms and popular idioms may be considered offensive:[77]

"Hey, Chief." If the American Indian addressed this way is not in fact a chief, this is considered insulting.

Squaw. For some Native people, this term is considered offensive, racist, and misogynistic. Depending on the tribe, the term translates to female sexual parts.[78]

"Hold down the fort." Historically, forts in America were built to hold back the Indians. To an American Indian, this implies that Indians are always on the "war path."

Pow-wow. In American Indian tradition, a pow-wow is a social gathering for ceremonial purposes. To refer to a quick meeting as a pow-wow trivializes that custom and could be offensive.

Low man on the totem pole. While this idiom might not be offensive, it could be considered insensitive. There is actually no hierarchy of importance connected with the images carved on totem poles.

Indian giver. This means that you give something away and then take it back. It is considered derogatory to American Indians. It may refer to the attempts by early settlers to buy land from American Indians, who at the time had no concept of land ownership and therefore did not understand that they were signing over their land.

Redskin. In 2022, Washington, DC's football team was renamed from the Redskins to the Commanders. Controversy and polarization has surrounded the team's name for years. *Redskin* is considered offensive and disrespectful because it was used throughout history in a pejorative way to describe American Indians. This derogatory slur is akin to calling a Black person the N-word.

Tribe. The use of the term *tribe* or phrase *find your tribe* is offensive because it negates the significance of tribal sovereignty and identity for American Indians. Instead use terms like group, community, circle, friends, or people.

Asian People in the United States

Here are phrases and questions to avoid and attitudes to watch out for when interacting with or speaking about Asian American people:[79]

"Where are you from?" When the answer is the United States, the secondary question is usually, "No, really, where

are you from originally?" The answer may still likely be
the United States. This question is offensive because it can
be interpreted as "You don't belong here" or "You are not as
American as I am."

"You speak good English." The implication here is that most
Asians do not speak "good" English.

*"Can you recommend a good Chinese/Indian/Thai/
Vietnamese/sushi restaurant?"* Just because a person is of
Asian descent does not mean he or she is an expert on
Asian food and restaurants.

Claims that Asians are not discriminated against because
they are prevalent in professional occupations, such as
doctors and IT professionals. In reality some Asian groups
earn the least amount of income in the United States.[80]

Assuming that Asian kids excel in school. This stereotype
is offensive because it is limiting and makes sweeping
generalizations about a group that may prevent students
from getting the help they need.

"You don't act very Asian." Again, this is a very stereotypical
comment. What is an Asian supposed to act like? Treat
people as individuals, not as a group stereotype.

"You all look alike." This may be the perception of someone
who has had limited exposure to different Asian cultures,
but it is another way of lumping together everyone from
one group, which ignores their individuality. (As mentioned
in Chapter 3, gaining more exposure and experience helps
one learn to differentiate.)

"Asians are not good leaders." There is a widespread
perception that Asians lack prototypical leadership traits.[81]
Asian employees who do not have Western roots might
have a different, quieter leadership style that is not as
valued in Western culture. (People with this mindset

might consider expanding their interpretation of desired leadership qualities.) As a result, many Asian people get "stuck" in middle management roles without getting credit for their vision and direction.[82]

"Why are you so quiet? You need to speak up more." This kind of mandate suggests the person requiring this behavior is not very culturally competent and isn't aware that there is more than one way to engage and that cultural behaviors vary. Rather than dictating new behaviors that fit the dominant cultural framework, strive to incorporate different methods of obtaining input.

Model minority. This designation, given to Asians because a large majority are seen as successful and highly educated, is still a gross generalization that overlooks the unique issues of inequality Asian Americans face. The Model Minority Mutiny movement is an attempt by the Asian American community to dispel the model minority myth in a show of solidarity with those who identify as BIPOC, and to acknowledge how this myth has been used to undercut Black civil rights efforts.[83]

Oriental. While it is not universally considered offensive, in the United States it is, at the very least, outdated. During his term, President Obama signed an order to eliminate the use of the term in all federal documents. Some opponents of the term believe it reinforces the perpetual foreigner stereotype often associated with Asian Americans, thus justifying exclusion of and discrimination against Asian Americans.[84] Asia is a very big continent that comprises numerous cultures. It is not useful to make sweeping generalities about Asians, or any group, for that matter. Learn to be specific and distinguish different cultural groups.

Referring to the coronavirus (COVID-19) as the "China virus." The 2020 coronavirus was referred to by some as the "China virus" due to the country of origin. Attaching a location or ethnicity to the disease creates a stigma that increases the unconscious (or conscious) bias against the associated identity group.

Latine People in the United States

Some triggering comments and questions for Latine workers include the following:

"You don't look Latine." We may have a preconceived notion of what someone from Latin America should look like. Latine people come from all different racial and ethnic groups and many different countries, and therefore there is no such thing as a Latine look.

"Do you speak Spanish?" or "Do you speak English?" The assumption that someone with a Latine heritage should speak Spanish is stereotypical, as is the assumption that the person may not speak English. Latine people may be second- or even third-generation Americans and may not speak Spanish. A Latine may be bilingual, speak only English, or speak only Spanish.

"Wow. Your English is so good." Why would you expect it not to be?

"Can you recommend a good landscaper or housekeeper?" The assumption is that most Latine individuals do landscaping or housekeeping work and therefore any Latine must know someone who does.

"I know a number of Mexican people." Not all Latines are Mexican. What message is the speaker trying to convey by saying this? That he or she understands the person being addressed? That he or she is not prejudiced? Claiming

to know Mexican people is probably irrelevant to the conversation.

"Tone it down. Why are you so emotional?" For some Latine cultures, animated discourse is a sign of enthusiasm and passion. For some Euro-American cultures, strong emotional expressiveness is seen as a distraction and inappropriate. (See Chapter 3.) Being told to tone it down can result in someone "shutting down."

"Do you speak Mexican?" Mexico is a country, not a language. Spanish is the official language of Mexico and most Latin American countries.

Illegal immigrant. As pointed out in Chapter 3, this term is offensive. It is labeling the person and not the action. It is judgmental language. There is still a presumption of innocence until a jury has convicted an individual.

White People

There are also sentiments that historically marginalized groups should avoid saying to white people, including the following:

"You could never understand my issues." While we have contended throughout the book that it is really hard to walk in another's shoes, there are many white people who do understand, want to understand, and want to be allies.

"All white people are racist." We are all biased, but we don't believe that all white people are racist—that they consciously believe that Black people and other historically marginalized groups are inferior and purposefully discriminate (take action) based on that belief.

"You are just a typical white person." What is a typical white person? This is a very stereotypical comment—a narrow,

limited perspective on an entire group of people. People are individuals.

"You are not diverse." Everyone is diverse. We are each unique. *Diverse* should not be an adjective to describe someone. Diversity is more than race—it is an intersection of identities, as we explored in Chapter 2 through the I Am exercise. It includes age, gender, gender identity, background, religion, sexual orientation, and so on. No two people are exactly alike. Two white men may be different in many ways—age, occupation, religion, geographic location, interests, and so on. All of these dimensions of diversity influence who we are.

"All white people are privileged." Privilege is relative. (See the discussion of privilege in Chapter 2.) We all have some level of privilege in various contexts. For example, there are Black people who have socioeconomic privilege over white people. To cast an entire group as privileged without knowing individual circumstances fuels polarization.

Gender

Gender inequity is a serious concern around the globe. While women make up half of the world's population, they continue to face serious inequities. In many organizations, women's upward mobility still lags; thus, the **glass ceiling** continues to persist.

According to a study by LeanIn.Org and McKinsey & Company, men significantly outnumber women at the manager level, with only 87 women for every 100 men being promoted from entry level to management, making it impossible to reach parity. By the time they reach the C-level, the numbers dwindle to only 1 in 4 women or 1 in 20 women of color making it to the C-suite.[85]

Here is a sampling of triggering comments and microinequities related to gender:

"Women are too emotional to be good leaders." Women may have learned to be more relationship oriented, to be nice, and to get along with others, while men may have learned to compete, to be brave, and not to cry. Men may have been socialized to believe they are supposed to protect women and not take direction from them. Contemporary research suggests that good leaders have a blend of qualities that includes emotional intelligence—being in touch with their own emotions and the emotions of others—making them more able to empathize and lead from the heart.

"Are you planning on having a family?" Asking this question may be cited as evidence of intent to discriminate if used to deny or limit work opportunities.[86]

"Work-life balance is a woman's issue." Work-life balance is a human issue. Both men and women must balance their work and personal responsibilities.

"Women are not as good in math or technical roles." This persistent stereotype is just not true. Men do not have more natural abilities in math and science. Studies show that the differential is due to social conditioning and the perpetuation of the stereotype.

"Women are not as committed to their careers." Gallup research suggests that women are actually more engaged than men in the workplace.[87]

When a woman speaks, her voice is often not heard. A man can offer the same input and be more likely to get recognition for the contribution. During President Obama's administration, high-ranking women were intentional about fixing this problem. They called it "amplification." They would repeat an idea of a female colleague and give her credit for the idea by name. The impact was that more women were being seen as valuable members of the team.[88]

Women are more likely to be judged by outward appearances than by their contributions. Research shows that "attractive" people—both men and women—earn higher salaries. Women, however, are held to an even higher standard. Throughout her political career, Hillary Clinton was often criticized for her dress and facial expressions. During a trip to Bangladesh in 2014, all of the media headlines focused on the fact that she decided to give a speech at Dhaka International School without makeup, rather than on the purpose of her talk.[89]

LGBTQIA+

Examples of comments that can be insensitive to the LGBTQIA+ community include the following:[90]

"I never would have guessed you were gay." While perhaps well intended, this comment has a judgmental tone. It could be interpreted as "I thought you were 'normal' like me."

"I suspected you were a lesbian." This type of comment plays into stereotypes and can come across with a judgmental and hurtful tone.

(To a transgender person) "What did you look like before?" or *"What was your name before?"* It is inappropriate to talk about past identity, presentation, names, and/or medical treatments if the person does not explicitly bring these up to you. Their current gender identity is who they are and should be affirmed.

"I have a gay friend that you should meet." No one should assume that a coworker would automatically want to meet their gay friend. Not all gay people are friends, just as not all straight people are friends.

"Your lifestyle is your business. We should not talk about that at work." Sexual orientation is not a choice the way a lifestyle is. The ability to bring one's whole self to work enhances engagement. Being able to include one's partner in office small talk or bringing the partner to work functions is part of being in an inclusive environment.

"I'm sorry." When spoken as a response to a coworker who has shared a part of their identity with you (such as being queer), this statement is judgmental. Why would you be sorry for that?

"What do gay people think about?" One gay person does not speak for the entire gay community. This is true for any of the groups discussed here. It is inappropriate to ask one person of a certain identity to speak for everyone in that group. Treat people as individuals. Another nuance here is expecting an LGBTQIA+ person to teach you things, for example, "Why does Sloane use they/them pronouns?" or "How is being bisexual different from being pansexual?" Google is your friend!

"Have you had the surgery yet?" Not your business! Imagine being asked about the exact state of your genitals at work and see if that's not weird.

"What are your preferred pronouns?" This question couches gender identity as a preference, rather than a deeply felt experience. It's okay—wonderful, in fact—to ask this question, just drop the word *preferred*.

"How did your family take it when you came out?" While many LGBTQIA+ people may have complex experiences with acceptance by some family members, they probably don't want to discuss them in casual conversation, and asking about them can reinforce a sense of othering.

"Using they/them for a single person isn't grammatically correct." Actually, singular they/them has been used for centuries! Many style books have more recently added this as an acceptable usage, and chances are you use it this way all the time when you don't know someone's gender. For example: "Someone left their wallet on the train."

Disability

We often shy away from discussing disabilities, mostly due to our fear of offending. People with disabilities have struggled to move beyond being depicted as one-dimensional sources of inspiration who offer others an opportunity to be heroically inclusive. They are more likely to be invisible and under-recognized for their capabilities and contributions. The stigma surrounding disability leads many people and their allies to be reluctant to self-identify, even if they need a workplace accommodation. It is well documented that people with disabilities are much more likely to be unemployed or underemployed. The latest data from the Bureau of Labor Statistics highlights the employment situation of people with and without disabilities in 2021. Only 21.3 percent of Americans age sixteen and over with disabilities were working or actively looking for work, far below the 67.1 percent rate for Americans without disabilities.[91]

Here are some microinequities and triggering words and phrases for people with disabilities:[92]

"What is wrong with you?" While this may be a well-intentioned question in an effort to be supportive, it is offensive. The term *wrong* is negative, and the opposite is *right*, so it connotes that the person is not legitimate. It is especially inappropriate if you do not know the person well and have not built a trusting relationship. Some people with disabilities

would prefer not to talk about their conditions. In order to engage in an inclusive conversation, it would be better to ask if the person would like to talk about his or her disability. If the answer is yes, the person with the disability should decide what they would like to share about the condition, and the person who asked should just listen. (See Chapter 5.)

"Were you born that way?" The person with a disability may wonder, "Was I born what way?" This can be an intrusive question, depending on the relationship. Again, it has a negative connotation.

"I don't think of you as a person with a disability." This is like saying I don't see you as a Black person or an Asian. We realize that often when someone says this, the intent is assurance of equality ("I don't see you as any different from me."). The person with a disability, however, may think, *Then you don't really see me. I am different, and that is okay.*

Speaking more slowly or loudly to a person in a wheelchair. Our unconscious biases may lead us to assume that a person in a wheelchair also has other limitations, and we might automatically respond by speaking more loudly or more slowly. Catch yourself if you do this. It is a part of the introspection and reflection process that we have discussed throughout the book.

Assuming that a person with a visible disability wants your help. As inclusion allies, we want to be helpful. Don't assume; ask the person if and how you can be helpful.

"How do you go to the bathroom?" This is also a very intrusive question. Even if someone is trying to learn more about the other person, as is advised in Chapter 3, this would probably not be a good question to pursue. It is private and personal and may make the other person feel very uncomfortable.

"You really look good." The implication here is surprise, as if a person with disabilities would not look good. Again, this probably well-intended statement is meant to be supportive, especially if someone has been out of work for a while with an illness. However, it can come across as, "You look good for someone in your condition." Or, the person might hear it as, "I really didn't have high expectations about how you would look." It might be better to say, "Good to have you back. Let me know if and how I can support you."

Expecting a neurodiverse person to only communicate your way or to change the way they communicate. Long email exchanges may be overwhelming and counterproductive for someone who is dyslexic, while someone with ADHD may not be able to respond right away if they are hyperfocused on another task. Similarly, someone with autism spectrum disorder may have difficulty maintaining eye contact due to how their neurodiverse brain works. While these effects and behaviors may not match up with neurotypical expectations, this does not mean neurodiverse colleagues are inherently flawed; like those with visible disabilities, their communication needs are just different and therefore require flexibility from neurotypical coworkers in order to bridge the gap.

Religion

Religion is a very difficult topic for the workplace. In general, ad hoc discussions about religion, like politics, should probably be avoided; however, structured conversations can help people to learn about each other's religions. A handful of major companies (e.g., American Express, Ford, and Google) have started faith-based employee resource groups.[93]

The Ford Interfaith Network (FIN) has been operating for more than two decades and is one of eleven company-approved employee groups. Its board members represent eight faiths—Buddhism, Catholicism, Judaism, Evangelical Christian, Islam, Hinduism, Orthodox Christianity, and the Church of Jesus Christ of Latter-day Saints. There are also "Other Affiliates," including Asatru, Baháʼí Faith, Humanism, Sikhism, Jainism, Spiritism, Paganism, Unitarianism, Zoroastrianism, and Universalism. All are welcome to join.[94] The primary purpose of faith-based employee resource groups is to educate employees about religious diversity. Companies believe that such networks can also help with recruitment and increase employee engagement.

The coordinated efforts to educate employees about different religious beliefs is a positive step. However, we still must be mindful of discussions and policies that are not inclusive.

Proselytizing. It is totally inappropriate for employees to try to convert others to their religion.

Denigrating someone else's religion. While you may totally disagree with someone else's beliefs, you should respect that they have the right to them.

Offering prayer or some other spiritual practice to someone who is not interested in it. We have to know when to keep our religious beliefs to ourselves and not force them on to others.

Generally Speaking

In general, for any group, if you want to increase the likelihood of having an effective Bold, Inclusive Conversation, you should avoid these types of phrases:

"I think you are being overly sensitive." How would you know? If you have not had the experience, you cannot judge the other person's response. Doing so is demeaning and dismissive. It is better to ask, "Why is this important to you?"

"That's not anything to worry about." Perhaps it is not
anything for you to worry about, but you cannot know what
the other person's reason for worrying might be.

"I know how you feel." You really don't know how someone
else feels. It is better to say, "Help me to understand how
that makes you feel."

"Calm down." This can be triggering for someone who
doesn't feel that they are being overly emotional. It might
be better to say, "I see that you have a lot of passion around
this topic." However, if the person is visibly angry, it might
be best to say, "Let's talk about this tomorrow after we have
both had an opportunity to think about it more."

"I have a lot of friends who are (fill in any group)." This is
offensive because it implies that because you have friends
from the same racial, ethnic, or religious group as the
person you're addressing, you could not be biased.

FINAL THOUGHTS: PUT YOUR HEART IN IT AND COMMIT TO LIVE INCLUSIVELY

We will never have all the right answers of what to say or
what to do when we are attempting Bold, Inclusive Conversations. There is usually more than one right answer, which
is what makes this work hard.

This book is a guide; the work is a journey. Don't try to
memorize all the dos and don'ts. If your heart is in the right
place and you genuinely have a desire to learn how to have
tough conversations on the topics that polarize our society, you will be fine. You will make mistakes along the way
because learning by its very definition is about making mistakes. Hopefully we will all learn the skill of patience to allow
more of us to grow together in our quest to make this a more
inclusive world.

We invite you to commit to live inclusively by sharing and signing the pledge below and inviting others to do the same!

COMMITMENT TO LIVE INCLUSIVELY

I commit to be intentional in living inclusively.

I commit to spending more time getting to know myself and understanding my culture. It is in understanding myself that I am better positioned to understand others. **I will** acknowledge that I don't know what I don't know, but I will not use what is unconscious as an excuse.

I will be intentional in exposing myself to difference. If I don't know, I will ask. If I am asked, I will assume positive intent. Most importantly, I will accept my responsibility in increasing my own knowledge and understanding.

I commit to speaking up and speaking out, even when I am not directly impacted, for there is no such thing as neutrality in the quest for equity, justice, and inclusion.

I will strive to accept, and not just tolerate; respect, even if I don't agree; and be curious, not judgmental. I commit to pausing and listening. I will be empathetic to the experiences and perspectives of my "others." I will use my privilege positively and get comfortable with my own discomfort.

I commit to knowing, getting, and doing better than I did yesterday—keeping in mind that my commitment to live inclusively is a journey, not a destination.

Your signature: _____

CHAPTER 8 ◆ TIPS FOR TALKING ABOUT IT!

◆ There are inclusive habits that you should hone and practice on a regular basis.

◆ Avoid words and phrases that may be offensive, insensitive, or outdated as you learn to converse with different groups.

◆ Don't try to memorize a list of dos and don'ts; they are a moving target and there is always more than one right answer.

◆ Think about what topics you find most difficult to have conversations about and commit to learning more about those issues and/or identity groups.

◆ Come from your heart, learn from your mistakes, and commit to continuing to contribute to making this a more inclusive world for all.

◆ Take and share the pledge to live inclusively!

◆ Invite others to take the pledge to live inclusively!

WE CAN'T TALK ABOUT THAT AT WORK!
Second Edition
◆ ◆ ◆
Discussion Guide

CHAPTER 1

1. How do you think external events impact people's ability to do their best work?

2. What is the best way to create psychologically safe spaces for employees to discuss polarizing topics?

3. There are so many external events happening today that can impact workers. How do you create space on an ongoing basis to address the emotional toll this takes on people?

4. Consider that events will impact different identity groups in different ways. How do you honor and respect those differences?

5. What tools and resources are helpful to support workers during stressful times?

CHAPTER 2

1. What are some of the key reasons that we do not talk about race, religion, politics, and other polarizing topics?
2. What are your I Ams (e.g., race, ethnicity, gender, gender identity, marital status, parental status, geographic region, religion, political affiliation, etc.)?
3. What aspects of your identity are most important to you? Why?
4. How do your important I Ams influence your values and beliefs?
5. How does a minimization mindset help us to have Bold, Inclusive Conversations? How does it hinder us from doing so?
6. How can you acknowledge the role that power and privilege play in your ability to have effective Bold, Inclusive Conversations?

CHAPTER 3

1. Most of us primarily have social networks composed of people from our own social identity. How do we expand beyond our comfort zone to expand our networks?
2. What are some ways you can practice the 4-Es inside and outside of the workplace?
3. What are some ways that we can assume positive intent when someone makes a mistake and says something offensive to us?
4. What does it mean to call someone "in" versus "calling them out"?

5. What are some ways to hold people accountable for inappropriate comments and behaviors?

6. What norms can you develop as a team to engage in difficult conversations where the harmed person does not always feel the burden of teaching?

7. What are some ways to build trust so that we can have authentic, open conversations?

8. Is your organization ready for Bold, Inclusive Conversations? Discuss the checklist (Chapter 3).

9. Are you ready for Bold, Inclusive Conversations? Discuss the Readiness Self-Assessment (Chapter 3).

CHAPTER 4

1. Why is the Why, Who, How, What, Where, and When model important to consider when engaging in Bold, Inclusive Conversations?

2. In today's more hybrid work environment, how will you decide if the gathering should be in person, virtual, or hybrid?

3. What are the pros and cons of in-person versus virtual or hybrid sessions?

4. What are ways to avoid spontaneous, unplanned conversations?

CHAPTER 5

1. How will you know that you are ready to pursue a conversation like Rodney and Jake's?

2. How do you know when you should bring in outside counsel from HR or legal?

3. What should you consider as you prepare for a conversation like Rodney and Jake's?

4. It can be difficult not to want to solve (bring closure to) a situation such as Rodney and Jake's in one meeting. What are the advantages of "pausing" to reflect and learn and scheduling another meeting to continue the conversation?

5. What are some ways to enhance our capability to listen to understand rather than listen to respond or defend?

6. What are some ways to get to shared meaning? Explore Are You Ready to Get to Shared Meaning? (Chapter 5).

7. Select a scenario. Practice using the Ladder of Inference to reach shared meaning (Chapter 5).

8. How can you integrate Bold, Inclusive Conversations into existing processes?

CHAPTER 6

1. How will you know when you are ready to continue a conversation like Rodney and Jake's?

2. What is the most difficult part of the conversation process?

3. Why is it important to define and clarify terms? What should you do if there are different interpretations?

4. What are the key signs for knowing when to pause, or even not continue, a conversation?

5. Storytelling is a powerful learning tool. What are the pros and cons to storytelling and various stages of the conversation process?

6. What is reciprocal empathy, and why is it important for Bold, Inclusive Conversations?

CHAPTER 7

1. Where do Bold, Inclusive Conversations fit into your overall DEI learning strategy?
2. How do Bold, Inclusive Conversations align with your organizational vision, mission, and strategic goals?
3. In what ways can you/have you applied the Bold, Inclusive Conversations model within your organization?
4. What barriers do you see in applying the Bold, Inclusive Conversations model within your organization? How can you overcome those?
5. How do you prepare people to facilitate Bold, Inclusive Conversations?

CHAPTER 8

1. What from the list of inclusive habits (Chapter 8) resonates most with you?
2. Define microinequities or microaggressions. How do they impede the ability to have Bold, Inclusive Conversations?
3. Name some key triggers for different identities that were outlined in the book. Which ones surprised you? Which ones have you experienced? What was missing from the lists?
4. How do you commit to live inclusively?

Glossary

Following are terms found throughout the book. For other helpful definitions, check out this resource from Racial Equity Tools: racialequitytools.org/glossary.

ableism: Beliefs or practices that rest on the assumption that being able-bodied is "normal" while other states of being need to be "fixed" or altered.

acceptance: An ethnorelative mindset on the Intercultural Development Continuum where individuals recognize and appreciate patterns of cultural difference and commonality in their own and other cultures.

accommodation style: An intercultural conflict style preferred by many Asian cultures and characterized as indirect and emotionally restrained.

adaptation: An ethnorelative orientation on the Intercultural Development Continuum that is capable of shifting cultural perspective and changing behavior in culturally appropriate and authentic ways. Adaptation involves both deep cultural bridging across diverse communities and an increased repertoire of cultural frameworks and practices to draw on in reconciling cultural commonalities and differences.

antiracism: The active process of identifying and eliminating racism by changing systems, organizational structures, policies and practices, and attitudes, so that power is redistributed and shared equitably.

antisemitism: Hostility to or prejudice against Jewish people.

BIPOC: Acronym for Black, Indigenous, and people of color; used to convey unity in the face of shared experiences while recognizing that every identity has a unique history with racism.

cancel culture: The mass withdrawal of support from public figures or celebrities who have done socially unacceptable things. This practice of "canceling" or mass shaming often occurs on social media platforms.

cisgender: Denotes a person whose gender identity corresponds with the sex registered for them at birth.

Civil Rights Act of 1964: The landmark civil rights and labor law in the United States that outlaws discrimination based on race, color, religion, sex, or national origin.

code-switching: The ways in which a member of a historically excluded group consciously or unconsciously adjusts the way they speak, behave, and appear to fit in with the dominant culture.

critical race theory: A term coined in the late 1980s by scholar Kimberlé Crenshaw, who sought to understand why laws were not working as intended to create equity for Black and other Indigenous people. Critical race theory is a way to study the enduring racial inequities in the United States and ask the question *Why?*

cultural humility: The ability to maintain an interpersonal stance that is other-oriented (or open to the other) in relation to aspects of the person's most important cultural identity.

cultural identity: A feeling or sense of belonging to a specific social group (nationality, ethnicity, religion, class, generation, etc.) that has its own distinct culture. Cultural identity can be characteristic of the individual or shared characteristics among group members.

culture: Shared beliefs, social norms, and traits of a social group, or a set of shared attitudes, values, goals, and practices that characterize an organization.

denial: A mindset on the Intercultural Development Continuum that reflects less capability for understanding and responding appropriately to cultural differences. Individuals with a denial orientation often do not recognize differences in perceptions and behavior as cultural. A denial orientation is characteristic of individuals who have limited experience with other cultural groups and therefore tend to operate with broad stereotypes and generalizations about the cultural other.

disability: A condition or function that results in challenges associated with performing daily life activities such as walking, seeing, or hearing.

discussion style: An intercultural conflict style characterized as direct and emotionally restrained. This style is most preferred by Euro-American, Northern European, and Canadian cultures.

dominant culture group: A group with systemic power, privileges, and social status within a society. Dominant does not imply majority. In the US context, dominant groups include white, male, heterosexual identities.

dynamic style: An intercultural conflict style common among SWANA cultures, characterized as indirect and emotionally expressive.

education (one of the 4-Es): Gaining new knowledge and skills through instruction, study, and experiences.

empathy (one of the 4-Es): The experience of understanding another person's condition from their perspective. You place yourself in their shoes and feel what they are feeling.

engagement style: An intercultural conflict style characterized as direct and emotionally expressive, most commonly found among African Americans, Greeks, some Western Europeans, and Latine cultures.

equity: Making sure people get access to the same opportunities by taking into consideration different needs based on past discrimination that continues to cause disparate outcomes.

ethnocentric worldview: A mindset/orientation that assumes the worldview of our own culture is central to reality. (See also denial and polarization.)

ethnorelative: A mindset that supposes cultures can only be understood relative to one another, and that particular behaviors can only be understood within a cultural context. (See also acceptance and adaptation.)

experience (one of the 4-Es): The extent to which one has intimately encountered, engaged with, and gained knowledge from being exposed to difference.

exposure (one of the 4-Es): The extent to which one comes into contact with cultural differences and diversity.

glass ceiling: A metaphor used to represent an invisible barrier that keeps a given demographic (typically applied to women) from rising beyond a certain level in a hierarchy.

heterosexual: A person who is sexually or romantically attracted exclusively to people of the opposite sex.

historically marginalized and excluded groups: Societal groups that have been traditionally oppressed, excluded, or disadvantaged.

hybrid work: A flexible work model that supports a blend of working in an office environment and working from home.

Intercultural Conflict Style Inventory: A cross-culturally validated assessment of an individual's approach to communicating, resolving conflicts, and solving problems.

Intercultural Development Continuum: A theoretical framework that ranges from the more monocultural mindsets of denial and polarization through the transitional orientation of minimization to the intercultural or global mindsets of acceptance and adaptation.

intersectionality: A term coined by scholar Kimberlé Crenshaw that describes the study of intersecting social identities (race, gender, class, etc.) and related systems of oppression. Intersectionality theory posits that multiple identities/isms are not mutually exclusive; rather, they intersect to create unique experiences.

Ladder of Inference: Describes the thinking process that we go through, usually without realizing it, to get from a fact to a decision or action. The thinking stages can be seen as rungs on a ladder.

Latine: Created by LGBTQIA+ Spanish speakers, this term adopts the letter *e* from the Spanish language to represent a gender-neutral alternative to Latino or Latina.

LGBTQIA+: An acronym that originated in the 1990s and replaced the phrase *gay community*. LGBTQIA+ stands for lesbian, gay, bisexual, transgender, queer (and/or questioning), intersex, asexual individuals/identities and was created to be more inclusive of diverse groups. The plus sign refers to the wide variety of gender identifications and sexual identities, which are expressed in terms that continue to evolve.

marginalized: Treated as insignificant or peripheral.

microaggression: Indirect, subtle, and sometimes unintentional discrimination against members of a marginalized group.

microinequities: Subtle, often unconscious, messages that single out, overlook, ignore, or otherwise discount individuals or groups based on aspects of their social identities (e.g., race, gender).

minimization: A transitional mindset on the Intercultural Development Continuum that highlights cultural commonality and universal values and principles that can mask a deeper understanding and consideration of cultural differences. Minimization can take one of two forms: (1) the highlighting of similarities due to limited cultural self-awareness, which is more commonly experienced by dominant group members within a cultural community; or (2) the highlighting of similarities more deliberatively as a strategy for navigating the values and practices largely determined by the dominant culture group, which is more commonly experienced by nondominant group members within a larger cultural community.

minoritize: To make a person or group subordinate in status to a more dominant group or its members.

multipartiality: A practice that supports facilitators in giving equal attention to multiple identities and experiences. Most importantly, it supports facilitators in giving attention to those identities and experiences that might be absent or unheard.

oppress: To keep someone in subservience and hardship, especially by the unjust exercise of authority.

Oriental: An outdated term used to describe people from East Asia. Now considered offensive by many when referencing people rather than objects.

platinum rule: An alternative to the widely known golden rule. The platinum rule encourages us to "Do unto others as they'd like done unto them."

polarization: An orientation on the Intercultural Development

Continuum that reflects a judgmental mindset that views cultural differences from an "us-versus-them" perspective. Polarization can take the form of defense ("My cultural practices are superior to other cultural practices") or reversal ("Other cultures are better than mine"). Within defense, cultural differences are often perceived as divisive and threatening to our own cultural way of doing things; reversal is a mindset that values and may idealize other cultural practices while denigrating those of our own culture group. Reversal may also support the cause of an oppressed group, but this is done with little knowledge of what the cause means to people from the oppressed community.

privilege: A social theory that posits special rights or advantages are available only to a particular person or group of people. The term is commonly used in the context of social inequality, particularly in regard to age, disability, ethnic or racial category, gender, sexual orientation, religion, and/or social class.

psychological safety: Feeling free to speak up about ideas, opinions, and challenges you are encountering, without fear of punishment or humiliation.

racialize: To make racial in tone or character, or to categorize or divide according to race.

reciprocal learning/mentoring: An instructional model where the traditional roles of mentor/coach and student/mentee are shared between the pair.

reverse mentoring: A process in which an individual in a dominant group learns from someone in a nondominant group (e.g., a white male learns from an African American, or a baby boomer learns from a millennial).

SWANA: A decolonized term for the South West/Asian/North African region that was created by its own community members.

unconscious bias: An unconscious judgment that happens automatically and is triggered by our brain making quick assessments of people and situations, influenced by our background, cultural environment, and personal experiences.

Notes

Introduction

1. Vanesha McGee, "Latino, Latinx, Hispanic, or Latine? Which Term Should You Use?," BestColleges, July 9, 2023, https://www.bestcolleges.com /blog/hispanic-latino-latinx-latine/.
2. "About," SWANA Alliance, accessed July 9, 2023, https://swanaalliance .com/about.
3. David Lanham and Amy Liu, "Not Just a Typographical Change: Why Brookings Is Capitalizing Black," Brookings, September 23, 2019, https:// www.brookings.edu/articles/brookingscapitalizesblack/.
4. Greg Iacurci, "2022 Was the 'Real Year of the Great Resignation,' Says Economist," *CNBC*, February 1, 2023, https://www.cnbc.com/2023/02/01 /why-2022-was-the-real-year-of-the-great-resignation.html.

CHAPTER 1

Epigraph: Peter Bromberg, email to Gabrielle Gayagoy Gonzalez, October 23, 2023.

5. Emma A. Renström, Hanna Bäck, and Royce Carroll, "Threats, Emotions, and Affective Polarization," *Political Psychology*, May 24, 2023, https:// doi.org/10.1111/pops.12899.
6. Khorri Atkinson, "Affirmative Action Ruling Sets Up Clash over Workplace Diversity," *Bloomberg Law*, June 30, 2023, https://news.bloomberg law.com/daily-labor-report/affirmative-action-ruling-sets-up-clash-over -workplace-diversity.
7. Kimmy Yam, "Anti-Asian Hate Crimes Increased 339 Percent Nationwide Last Year, Report Says," *NBC News*, January 31, 2022, https://www

.nbcnews.com/news/asian-america/anti-asian-hate-crimes-increased-339
-percent-nationwide-last-year-repo-rcna14282.

8. Geoff Bennett and Karina Cuevas, "Anti-Defamation League Reports
Dramatic Rise in Antisemitism in US," *PBS News Hour*, March 23, 2023,
https://www.pbs.org/newshour/show/anti-defamation-league-reports
-dramatic-rise-in-antisemitism-in-u-s.

9. "Roe v Wade: US Firms Pledge to Pay Staff Travel Expenses for Abortions," *BBC*, June 26, 2022, https://www.bbc.com/news/business-61941591.

10. "2023 Anti-Trans Bills Tracker," Trans Legislation Tracker, accessed
August 2, 2023, https://translegislation.com/.

11. Sarah Schwartz, "Map: Where Critical Race Theory Is under Attack,"
Education Week, June 13, 2023, https://www.edweek.org/policy-politics
/map-where-critical-race-theory-is-under-attack/2021/06.

12. "FBI Releases Supplement to the 2021 Hate Crime Statistics," United
States Department of Justice, accessed August 2, 2023, https://www.justice
.gov/crs/highlights/2021-hate-crime-statistics.

13. Clyde McGrady and Emily Cochrane, "'The Justins' Follow a Legacy
of Resistance in Tennessee," *New York Times*, April 17, 2023, https://www
.nytimes.com/2023/04/14/us/justin-pearson-justin-jones-tennessee.html.

14. "State of the American Workplace: Employee Engagement Insights for
US Business Leaders," Gallup, accessed January 31, 2017, https://news.gallup
.com/opinion/gallup/170570/gallup-releases-new-findings-state-american
-workplace.aspx.

15. Jeanine Prime and Elizabeth R. Salib, "The Secret to Inclusion in Australian Workplaces: Psychological Safety," Catalyst, accessed August 25, 2015,
https://www.catalyst.org/research/the-secret-to-inclusion-in-australian
-workplaces-psychological-safety/.

16. Hard News: Journalists and the Threat of Disinformation," PEN
America, accessed October 23, 2023, https://pen.org/report/hard-news
-journalists-and-the-threat-of-disinformation/.

17. "2023 Gen Z and Millennial Survey," Deloitte, accessed September
20, 2023, https://www.deloitte.com/global/en/issues/work/content/genz
millennialsurvey.html.

18. Curtis Bunn, "Hamstrung by 'Golden Handcuffs': Diversity Roles
Disappear 3 Years after George Floyd's Murder Inspired Them," *NBC News*,
February 27, 2023, https://www.nbcnews.com/news/nbcblk/diversity-roles
-disappear-three-years-george-floyd-protests-inspired-rcna72026.

19. Shawn Shinneman, "'Tolerance Is for Cowards'...AT&T CEO Randall
Stephenson Speaks on Racial Tension and Black Lives Matter," *Dallas Business Journal*, October 3, 2016, http://www.bizjournals.com/dallas/blog
/techflash/2016/10/tolerance-is-for-cowards-at-t-ceo-randall.html.

20. Jeremie Brecheisen, "Research: Where Employees Think Companies'
DEIB Efforts Are Failing," *Harvard Business Review*, March 9, 2023, https://

hbr.org/2023/03/research-where-employees-think-companies-deib-efforts
-are-failing.

CHAPTER 2

Epigraph: Ralph Ellison, *Invisible Man* (New York: Random House, 1952), 232.
   21. Erik Homburger Erikson, *Identity: Youth and Crisis* (London: Faber & Faber, 1968).
   22. Caryn J. Block, Sandy M. Koch, Benjamin E. Liberman, Tarani J. Merriweather, and Loriann Roberson, "Contending with Stereotype Threat at Work: A Model of Long-Term Responses 1–7," *The Counseling Psychologist* 39, no. 4 (2011): 570–600.
   23. The Intercultural Development Inventory can be found at www.idiinventory.com.
   24. Marianne Williamson, *A Return to Love* (New York: HarperCollins Press, 2009).
   25. Heather McGhee, *The Sum of Us: What Racism Costs Everyone and How We Can Prosper Together* (New York: One World, 2021).

CHAPTER 3

Epigraph: Mellody Hobson, "Color Blind or Color Brave?" TED Talks, May 5, 2014, https://www.ted.com/talks/mellody_hobson_color_blind_or_color_brave?
   26. Mellody Hobson, "Color Blind or Color Brave?" TED Talks, accessed January 27, 2017, https://www.ted.com/talks/mellody_hobson_color_blind_or_color_brave.
   27. "American Bubbles: Politics, Race, and Religion in Americans' Core Friendship Networks," Public Religion Research Institute, May 24, 2022, https://www.prri.org/research/american-bubbles-politics-race-and-religion-in-americans-core-friendship-networks/.
   28. Luis Romero and Saher Selod, "Surveillance and the Consequences of Perceiving Muslims as Anti-American," Public Religion Research Institute, June 3, 2022, https://www.prri.org/spotlight/surveillance-and-the-consequences-of-perceiving-muslims-as-anti-american/.
   29. Besheer Mohamed, "Muslims Are a Growing Presence in US, but Still Face Negative Views from the Public," Pew Research Center, September 1, 2021.
   30. "How to Measure Employee Engagement With the Q12," Gallup, accessed September 20, 2023, https://www.gallup.com/workplace/356045/q12-question-summary.aspx.
   31. Sylvia Ann Hewlett, Maggie Jackson, and Ellis Cose with Courtney Emerson, "Vaulting the Color Bar: How Sponsorship Levers Multicultural Professionals into Leaders," Coqual, formerly Center for Talent Innovation,

accessed September 20, 2023, https://coqual.org/wp-content/uploads/2020 /09/36_vaultingthecolorbar_keyfindings-1.pdf.

32. Junot Díaz, *The Brief Wondrous Life of Oscar Wao* (New York: Riverhead Books, 2007).

33. "Race Reporting Guide: A Race Forward Media Reference," Race Forward Center for Racial Justice Innovation, accessed January 25, 2017, https://www.raceforward.org/sites/default/files/Race%20Reporting%20Guide %20by%20Race%20Forward_V1.1.pdf.

34. Sapna Maheshwari, "Top Estée Lauder Executive Forced Out for Racist Instagram Post," *New York Times*, February 28, 2022, https://www.nytimes .com/2022/02/28/business/estee-lauder-john-demsey-ousted.html.

35. "Company Update from William P. Lauder and Fabrizio Freda," Estée Lauder Companies, February 28, 2022, https://www.elcompanies.com/en /news-and-media/newsroom/company-features/2022/company-update -john-demsey.

36. Brenton Blanchet, "Chingy Responds to Racist Meme Shared by Estée Lauder Exec That Referenced the Rapper and 'Sesame Street,'" *Complex*, March 1, 2022, https://www.complex.com/music/a/b-blanchet/chingy -not-concerned-after-trending-over-estee-lauder-exec-racist-seasme-street -meme.

37. Jenny B. Fine, "John Demsey's Career High," *Women's Wear Daily*, May 14, 2021, https://wwd.com/feature/john-demseys-career-high-1234821487/.

38. Rashad Grove, "Estée Lauder Executive John Demsey Suspended After Posting a Racially Insensitive Instagram Post," *Ebony*, February 25, 2022, https://www.ebony.com/estee-lauder-executive-john-demsey-instagram -controversy/.

39. Jennifer Hassan, "Whoopi Goldberg Suspended From 'The View' After Claim Holocaust Was 'Not About Race,'" *Washington Post*, February 1, 2022, https://www.washingtonpost.com/lifestyle/2022/02/01/whoopi-goldberg -holocaust-race-apology/.

40. "Whoopi Goldberg Suspended from 'The View' for 2 Weeks over Holocaust Comments," *ABC News*, February 1, 2022, https://abcnews.go.com /US/whoopi-goldberg-suspended-view-weeks-holocaust-comments/story ?id=82613265.

41. "About the ICS Inventory," Intercultural Conflict Style Inventory (ICS), accessed September 20, 2023, https://icsinventory.com/ics-inventory.

42. Sylvia Ann Hewlett, Melinda Marshall, and Laura Sherbin, "How Diversity Can Drive Innovation," *Harvard Business Review*, December 2013, https://hbr.org/2013/12/how-diversity-can-drive-innovation.

43. Paul J. Zak, "The Neuroscience of Trust," *Harvard Business Review*, January–February 2017, https://hbr.org/2017/01/the-neuroscience-of-trust.

44. Stephen M.R. Covey, *The Speed of Trust: The One Thing That Changes Everything* (New York: Simon and Schuster, 2006).

45. Thomas Kochman, *Black and White Styles in Conflict* (Chicago: University of Chicago Press, 1981).

46. Maya Angelou, posted on official Twitter account, now known as X, May 12, 2013, https://twitter.com/DrMayaAngelou/status/33360957868 6197760.

CHAPTER 4

47. "8 Ways Remote Work Has Changed since the Pandemic," G-P, accessed September 20, 2023, https://www.globalization-partners.com/resources/ways-remote-work-changed-since-pandemic/.

48. "The Impact of Covid-19 on Workplace Inclusion: Survey," Catalyst, July 15, 2020, https://www.catalyst.org/research/workplace-inclusion-covid-19.

49. Nurcan Karamolla Ensari and Norman Miller, "The Application of the Personalization Model in Diversity Management," *Group Processes & Intergroup Relations*, 9(4), 589–607, https://doi.org/10.1177/1368430206067679.

50. "The Impact of Covid-19 on Workplace Inclusion: Survey," Catalyst, July 15, 2020, https://www.catalyst.org/research/workplace-inclusion-covid-19.

51. Leon Yin and Aaron Sankin, "How We Uncovered Disparities in Internet Deals," The Markup, October 19, 2022, https://themarkup.org/show-your-work/2022/10/19/how-we-uncovered-disparities-in-internet-deals.

52. "Gartner Forecasts 39% of Global Knowledge Workers Will Work Hybrid by the End of 2023," Gartner, March 1, 2023, https://www.gartner.com/en/newsroom/press-releases/2023-03-01-gartner-forecasts-39-percent-of-global-knowledge-workers-will-work-hybrid-by-the-end-of-2023.

53. "Black, Hispanic Americans Are Overrepresented in Essential Jobs," University of Illinois Chicago, February 2, 2021, https://publichealth.uic.edu/news-stories/black-hispanic-americans-are-overrepresented-in-essential-jobs/.

54. "Caucuses as a Racial Justice Strategy: What We Have Learned," JustLead Washington, July 2019, https://justleadwa.org/wp-content/uploads/2019/07/Caucuses-as-a-Racial-Justice-Strategy-JustLead-WA.pdf.

CHAPTER 5

Epigraph: Roy T. Bennett, *The Light in the Heart* (Roy Bennett, 2016).

55. "Prisoners in 2021," Bureau of Justice Statistics, December 2022, https://bjs.ojp.gov/sites/g/files/xyckuh236/files/media/document/p21st_sumB.pdf.

56. Curtis Bunn, "Report: Black People Are Still Killed by Police at a Higher Rate Than Other Groups," *NBC News*, March 3, 2022, https://www

.nbcnews.com/news/nbcblk/report-black-people-are-still-killed-police
-higher-rate-groups-rcna17169.

57. United States Census Bureau, "QuickFacts," accessed September 20,
2023, https://www.census.gov/quickfacts/fact/table/US/PST045222.

58. "Jail Inmates in 2021," Bureau of Justice Statistics, December 2022,
https://bjs.ojp.gov/library/publications/jail-inmates-2021-statistical-tables.

59. Howard Zinn, *A People's History of the United States* (New York:
Harper Perennial Modern Classics, 2015).

60. Nell Irvin Painter, *The History of White People* (New York: W. W.
Norton & Company, 2011).

61. Mark Peffley and Jon Hurwitz, *Justice in America: The Separate Realities of Blacks and Whites* (Cambridge: Cambridge University Press, 2010).

62. Michelle Alexander, *The New Jim Crow: Mass Incarceration in the Age
of Colorblindness* (New York: The New Press, 2020).

63. Ibram X. Kendi, *Stamped from the Beginning: The Definitive History of
Racist Ideas in America* (New York: Bold Type Books, 2016).

64. Mary-Frances Winters, *Black Fatigue: How Racism Erodes the Mind,
Body, and Spirit* (Oakland: Berrett-Koehler Publishers, 2020).

65. Heather McGhee, *The Sum of Us: What Racism Costs Everyone and
How We Can Prosper Together* (New York: One World, 2021).

66. *13th,* directed by Ava DuVernay, 2016, on Netflix, https://www
.netflix.com/title/80091741.

67. Chimamanda Ngozi Adichie, "The Danger of a Single Story," filmed
July 2009 at TEDGlobal, Oxford, UK, video, 17:24, https://www.ted
.com/talks/chimamanda_ngozi_adichie_the_danger_of_a_single_story
?language=en.

CHAPTER 6

Epigraph: Morgan Harper Nichols, Facebook post, April 29, 2019, https://
www.facebook.com/morganharpernichols/photos/tell-the-story-of-the
-mountains-you-climbed-your-words-could-become-a-page-in-so/2301689
093407984/.

68. "Support for the Black Lives Matter Movement Varies by Race, Ethnicity, Age and Partisanship," Pew Research Center, accessed September 20,
2023, https://www.pewresearch.org/social-trends/2023/06/14/views-on
-the-black-lives-matter-movement/st_2023-06-14_blm-support_01_01/.

69. "Deep Divisions in Americans' Views of Nation's Racial History—and
How to Address It," Pew Research Center, August 12, 2021, https://www
.pewresearch.org/politics/2021/08/12/deep-divisions-in-americans-views
-of-nations-racial-history-and-how-to-address-it/.

70. "Report: Black People 7.5 Times More Likely to Be Wrongfully
Convicted of Murder Than Whites, Risk Even Greater if Victim Was White,"

Death Penalty Information Center, September 30, 2022, https://death penaltyinfo.org/news/report-black-people-7-5-times-more-likely-to-be -wrongfully-convicted-of-murder-than-whites-risk-even-greater-if-victim -was-white.

71. "2018 Crime in the United States," FBI Uniform Crime Reporting, accessed September 20, 2023, https://ucr.fbi.gov/crime-in-the-u.s/2018 /crime-in-the-u.s.-2018/tables/expanded-homicide-data-table-6.xls.

72. Shawn A. Ginwright, *The Four Pivots* (Berkeley: North Atlantic Books, 2022), 33.

CHAPTER 7

73. *Oxford Essential Quotations* (Oxford: Oxford University Press, 2017).

74. Leigh Morrison, "Managing the Toll of DEI Work: Understanding Your Triggers," The Inclusion Solution, January 30, 2020, https://the inclusionsolution.me/managing-the-toll-of-dei-work-understanding-your -triggers/.

75. Christopher Cardarelli, interview with Mareisha N. Reese, May 31, 2023.

76. "About Us: Diversity & Inclusion," Merck, accessed September 20, 2023, https://www.merck.com/company-overview/diversity-and -inclusion/.

CHAPTER 8

77. "Things NOT to Say to American Indian Coworkers," DiversityInc, accessed January 31, 2017, http://www.diversityinc.com/things-not-to-say /things-never-to-say-to-american-indian-coworkers/.

78. "Editorial Note: The Use of the Word Squaw," The Native Northeast Portal, accessed September 20, 2023, http://nativenortheastportal.com /editorial-note-use-word-squaw.

79. Stacy Straczynski, "7 Things NOT to Say to Asian-Americans," DiversityInc, accessed January 31, 2017, http://www.diversityinc.com/things-not -to-say/7-things-not-to-say-to-asian-americans/.

80. Abby Budiman and Neil G. Ruiz, "Key Facts about Asian Origin Groups in the US," Pew Research Center, April 29, 2021, https://www.pew research.org/short-reads/2021/04/29/key-facts-about-asian-origin-groups -in-the-u-s/.

81. Stefanie K. Johnson and Thomas Sy, "Why Aren't There More Asian Americans in Leadership Positions?" *Harvard Business Review*, December 19, 2016, https://hbr.org/2016/12/why-arent-there-more-asian-americans-in -leadership-positions#.

82. Jessica Guynn, "No Longer Suffering in Silence: Asian Americans Denied Tech Leadership Roles Go to Court," *USA Today*, July 6, 2023,

https://www.usatoday.com/story/money/2023/07/06/asian-americans
-denied-leadership-roles-tech-industry-lawsuit/70369457007/.

83. Soya Jung, "What Does Model Minority Mutiny Demand?" Race
Files, December 13, 2014, https://www.racefiles.com/2014/12/13/what-does
-model-minority-mutiny-demand/.

84. Jayne Tsuchiyama, "The Term 'Oriental' Is Outdated, but Is It Racist?"
Los Angeles Times, accessed January 31, 2017, http://www.latimes.com
/opinion/op-ed/la-oe-tsuchiyama-oriental-insult-20160601-snap-story
.html.

85. "Women in the Workplace 2022," LeanIn.Org and McKinsey &
Company, accessed September 20, 2023, https://leanin.org/women-in-the
-workplace/2022/were-in-the-midst-of-a-great-breakup.

86. "Pre-Employment Inquiries and Marital Status or Number of Children," US Equal Employment Opportunity Commission," accessed September
20, 2023, https://www.eeoc.gov/pre-employment-inquiries-and-marital
-status-or-number-children.

87. "State of the American Workplace: Employee Engagement Insights for
US Business Leaders," Gallup, June 11, 2013.

88. Keli Goff, "How the Women of the Obama White House Fought
Gender Inequality—and We Can Too," *Daily Beast*, April 13, 2017, https://
www.thedailybeast.com/how-the-women-of-the-obama-white-house-fought
-gender-inequalityand-we-can-too.

89. Eve Tahmincioglu, "For Women in the Workplace, It's Still about
Looks Not Deeds," *Today*, accessed January 25, 2017, http://www.today.com
/money/women-workplace-its-still-about-looks-not-deeds-772762.

90. Quispe López and Marguerite Ward, "12 Things You Should Never
Say to Your LGBTQ Coworkers," *Insider*, June 5, 2020, https://www.business
insider.com/lgbtq-workers-discrimination-things-not-to-say-2019-9.

91. Madison Hoff, "How Americans with Disabilities Are Underrepresented as Managers and Professionals, in One Glaring Chart," *Insider*,
February 28, 2022, https://www.businessinsider.com/chart-jobs-occupations
-people-with-disabilities-are-working-in-2022-2.

92. "7 Things Never to Say to People with Disabilities," DiversityInc,
accessed January 31, 2017, http://www.diversityinc.com/things-not-to-say
/7-things-never-to-say-to-people-with-disabilities/.

93. "Companies with Faith Based Employee Resource Groups," Faith
Driven Investor, accessed September 20, 2023, https://www.faithdriven
investor.org/information-on-companies-with-ergs.

94. "Ford Interfaith Network," Religious Freedom & Business Foundation, accessed August 2, 2023, https://religiousfreedomandbusiness.org/ford
-interfaith-network-fin.

Acknowledgments

We would like to acknowledge the entire Winters Group team for their passion and dedication in actualizing Bold, Inclusive Conversations in the workplace and community. We appreciate their thoughtful input as we worked on the second edition to ensure its continued relevance.

An extra special thanks to Gabrielle (Gabby) Gayagoy Gonzalez, The Winters Group marketing and PR strategist, who supported us as special projects editor for this second edition. Gabby's insight and attention to detail is unparalleled. Thank you for the countless hours you gave to us and your passion for diversity, equity, inclusion, and justice.

We also acknowledge Megan Ellinghausen, marketing and branding specialist at The Winters Group, for (re)creating the graphics included in this book. Thank you for your creative genius in marketing and branding The Winters Group's work.

Thank you to the readers of the first edition, and the facilitators and participants in our Engaging in Bold, Inclusive Conversations Facilitator Certification Program. We are grateful to you for advancing and implementing the concepts and tools in this book. You are true ambassadors for the Bold, Inclusive Conversations model.

Thank you to YOU, the reader. We hope you will take what you learn from these pages to help create a world where effective conversations around polarizing topics become the norm and not the exception. Thank you for your commitment to diversity, equity, and inclusion and for living and leading inclusively.

MAREISHA'S SPECIAL ACKNOWLEDGMENT

I have immense gratitude for Mary-Frances Winters, my business partner, coauthor, and, most important title, my mom. Thank you for affording me this opportunity to coauthor this second edition with you. I continue to learn so much from you daily as a thought leader in this field. The world is a greater place with your wisdom in it. You are greatly loved. Thank you.

Index

Page numbers followed by an "f" indicate a figure, and those followed by a "t" indicate a table.

About the Authors

Rae Images

Mary-Frances Winters (she/her/hers) is the founder and CEO of The Winters Group, Inc., a global diversity, equity, inclusion, and justice consulting firm started in 1984. She truly believes that diversity and inclusion work is her "passion and calling." A known thought leader in the field, she has for the past four decades impacted hundreds of organizations and thousands of individuals with her thought-provoking message and her approach to diversity and inclusion. Mary-Frances is a master strategist with experience in strategic planning, change management, diversity, organization development, training and facilitation, systems thinking, and qualitative and quantitative research methods. She has extensive experience in working with senior leadership teams to drive organizational change.

Among her many awards and distinctions, Mary-Frances was named a diversity pioneer by *Profiles in Diversity Journal* in 2007 and most recently received the journal's Black

Leadership Award in 2023. She is also the 2016 recipient of the Winds of Change award from the Forum on Workplace Inclusion. In addition, she was featured in *Forbes's* June 2016 publication, which honored some of the DC Metro area's most powerful women. In November 2019, Mary-Frances was named by *Forbes* as one of ten trailblazers in diversity and inclusion. She was accepted into the Forbes Business Council in 2023.

Mary-Frances has served as a torch bearer for the Olympics and has been recognized as an Athena Award winner from the Greater Rochester Chamber of Commerce for her contributions to women and the community.

In addition to *We Can't Talk about That at Work!* Mary-Frances is the author of six books: *Racial Justice at Work: Practical Solutions for Systemic Change; Black Fatigue: How Racism Erodes the Mind, Body, and Spirit; Inclusive Conversations: Fostering Equity, Empathy, and Belonging across Differences; Only Wet Babies Like Change: Workplace Wisdom for Baby Boomers; Inclusion Starts With "I": Eight Steps to Inclusion: The Personal Journey;* and *CEOs Who Get It: Diversity Leadership from the Heart and Soul.* Mary-Frances also authored a chapter in the book *Diversity at Work: The Practice of Inclusion* and numerous articles.

Mary-Frances is a graduate of the University of Rochester with undergraduate degrees in English and psychology, and a master's degree in business administration from the William E. Simon Executive Development Program. She received an honorary doctorate from Roberts Wesleyan College. She serves on the Board of Trustees of the University of Rochester, the Board of Visitors for Johnson C. Smith University, and The Council on Black Health.

Rae Images

Mareisha N. Reese (she/her/hers) is a Xennial (cusp of millennial and Generation X) Black woman who serves as president and chief operating officer at The Winters Group, Inc. In this role, Mareisha manages the day-to-day operations of the organization, ensuring it runs like a well-oiled machine. She joined the company in 2012 as vice president to help develop new products, bring in new business, service clients, manage social media, and research and consult.

Prior to joining The Winters Group, Mareisha worked as a software engineer for a large defense contractor. The experience of often being the only Black woman in her workspaces, and the biases and microaggressions that came along with that, led to her passion for diversity, equity, inclusion, and justice work. She took that passion to her role as program manager for HBCU-UP at Johnson C. Smith University, a National Science Foundation Grant–funded program to recruit, retain, and graduate underrepresented students in science, technology, engineering, and mathematics (STEM) fields.

Mareisha earned a bachelor of science in computer science from Spelman College, a bachelor of science in electrical engineering from Georgia Tech, and dual master's degrees in business administration and information systems from the University of Maryland Robert H. Smith School of Business. She was named to Diversity MBA's Top 100 Under 50 Executive and Emerging Leaders in 2021 and Diversity Woman Media's The Power 100 List in 2021. In 2023, Mareisha was recognized with a Women Worth Watching in Leadership Award from *Profiles in Diversity Journal* and the *Charlotte Business Journal* Power 100 for DEI. Mareisha is a coauthor of *Racial Justice at Work: Practical Solutions for Systemic Change.*

About The Winters Group, Inc.

The Winters Group, Inc. is a Black women–owned diversity, equity, inclusion, and justice (DEIJ) global consulting firm. Since 1984, The Winters Group has unapologetically challenged systems of oppression and pushed the boundaries of what it means to be inclusive. Our work is informed by the lived experiences of our team composed of more than 80 percent women and more than 70 percent BIPOC. Clients range from Fortune 100 companies, educational institutions, and nonprofit organizations, all of whom look to The Winters Group to relentlessly shepherd bold, fearless leadership that centers the experiences of the marginalized through our services, which include equity audits and assessments, strategy development and implementation, customized learning experiences, and executive coaching. For more information, visit wintersgroup.com.

Berrett–Koehler
Publishers

Berrett-Koehler is an independent publisher dedicated to an ambitious mission: *Connecting people and ideas to create a world that works for all.*

Our publications span many formats, including print, digital, audio, and video. We also offer online resources, training, and gatherings. And we will continue expanding our products and services to advance our mission.

We believe that the solutions to the world's problems will come from all of us, working at all levels: in our society, in our organizations, and in our own lives. Our publications and resources offer pathways to creating a more just, equitable, and sustainable society. They help people make their organizations more humane, democratic, diverse, and effective (and we don't think there's any contradiction there). And they guide people in creating positive change in their own lives and aligning their personal practices with their aspirations for a better world.

And we strive to practice what we preach through what we call "The BK Way." At the core of this approach is *stewardship,* a deep sense of responsibility to administer the company for the benefit of all of our stakeholder groups, including authors, customers, employees, investors, service providers, sales partners, and the communities and environment around us. Everything we do is built around stewardship and our other core values of *quality, partnership, inclusion,* and *sustainability.*

This is why Berrett-Koehler is the first book publishing company to be both a B Corporation (a rigorous certification) and a benefit corporation (a for-profit legal status), which together require us to adhere to the highest standards for corporate, social, and environmental performance. And it is why we have instituted many pioneering practices (which you can learn about at www.bkconnection.com), including the Berrett-Koehler Constitution, the Bill of Rights and Responsibilities for BK Authors, and our unique Author Days.

We are grateful to our readers, authors, and other friends who are supporting our mission. We ask you to share with us examples of how BK publications and resources are making a difference in your lives, organizations, and communities at www.bkconnection.com/impact.

Dear reader,

Thank you for picking up this book and welcome to the worldwide BK community! You're joining a special group of people who have come together to create positive change in their lives, organizations, and communities.

What's BK all about?

Our mission is to connect people and ideas to create a world that works for all.

Why? Our communities, organizations, and lives get bogged down by old paradigms of self-interest, exclusion, hierarchy, and privilege. But we believe that can change. That's why we seek the leading experts on these challenges—and share their actionable ideas with you.

A welcome gift

To help you get started, we'd like to offer you a **free copy** of one of our bestselling ebooks:

www.bkconnection.com/welcome

When you claim your **free ebook**, you'll also be subscribed to our blog.

Our freshest insights

Access the best new tools and ideas for leaders at all levels on our blog at ideas.bkconnection.com.

Sincerely,

Your friends at Berrett-Koehler